+HD30.28 .S39+

COLLEGE FOR HUMAN SERVICES
LI
345 HUDSON STREET
NEW YORK, N.Y. 10014

HOW TO PREPARE EFFECTIVE BUSINESS PROGRAM BLUEPRINTS

A MANAGEMENT HANDBOOK

David D. Seltz
President
Seltz Franchising
Developments, Inc.

▲ ADDISON-WESLEY PUBLISHING COMPANY
Reading, Massachusetts • Menlo Park, California
London • Amsterdam • Don Mills, Ontario • Sydney

Library of Congress Cataloging in Publication Data

Seltz, David D
   How to prepare effective business program blueprints.

   1. Corporate planning. I. Title.
HD30.28.S39   658.4'012   79-27209
ISBN 0-201-07618-7

Copyright © 1981 by David D. Seltz. Philippines copyright 1981 by David D. Seltz.

All rights reserved. No part of this publication may be reproduced, stored in a retrieval system, or transmitted, in any form or by any means, electronic, mechanical, photocopying, recording, or otherwise, without the prior written permission of the publisher. Printed in the United States of America. Published simultaneously in Canada. Library of Congress Catalog Card No. 79-27209.

ISBN 0-201-07618-7
ABCDEFGHIJ-AL-89876543210

PREFACE

Throughout this book there are frequent references to "blueprints." This word has been borrowed from the engineering and mechanical fields as a matter of convenience, and its connotation here is best described by Webster's secondary definition:

> ". . . a detailed, thoroughly coordinated plan or program of action . . ."

This is good usage, for the "business blueprint" is a carefully conceived and practical procedure for the implementation of various business plans of action. The blueprint has as its ultimate goal the assessment of the feasibility of such plans. In each case they ask:

- Can it be done?
- How can it be done?
- What is the plan's reasonable profitability?
- How long will it be before potential profits can be realized?
- How much working capital will be necessary?
- Can it be accomplished with present personnel?
- What is the competition?
- How large is the market?
- Should we undertake the plan?

PREFACE

The business blueprint is a basic analytical presentation of a business concept. It acts to codify, package, and implement preliminary unproved ideas, thereby avoiding expensive, time-consuming, trial-and-error processes. The techniques of constructing such a blueprint will be discussed step-by-step. Management executives will find that this planning method has wide application and is a great aid in arriving at a reliable business decision.

New York, New York D. D. S.
October 1980

CONTENTS

CHAPTER ONE WHAT THE BLUEPRINT DOES

It Plans Ahead 2
It Estimates Prospective Income Factors 2
It Analyzes 2

CHAPTER TWO THE NEED

Plan Now for Change Later 6
Some Changes that Might be Anticipated 6
Developing Options 9
Availability of New Markets 9
Need to Assess Current Trends 9
Innovation, Diversification, and Add-on
  Profit Centers 10

CHAPTER THREE THE PROCESS OF BLUEPRINT PREPARATION

Preparatory Steps 14
Evaluating Feasibility 18
Preparation of a Blueprint's Table of Contents 29

CHAPTER FOUR PROGRAM ARITHMETIC: EXAMINING THE BOTTOM LINE

The Arithmetic of Business—the Bottom Line 32
The Pro-Forma Cash Flow 38
The Pro-Forma Income Statement 39
The Break-Even Analysis 45
Capital Requirements 46
Additional Examples 48

CHAPTER FIVE EVALUATING FINANCE OPTIONS

Bank Loans 54
Government Financing 55
Other Avenues 58

CHAPTER SIX EVALUATING LOCATION REQUIREMENTS

Site Selection 62

CHAPTER SEVEN EVALUATING ADVERTISING AND PROMOTION

Advertising and Promotion 68
Pre-Opening and Grand-Opening Procedures 68
Effective Low-Budget Promotional Concepts 74
Take an Objective Look at Your Operation 80

CHAPTER EIGHT REQUIRED ORGANIZATION PERSONNEL

Organization 86
Personnel Acquisition and Organization
    Charts 89

Evaluating Job Responsibilities 95
Table of Organization 97
Field Supervision 103

CHAPTER NINE OPTIONAL FORMS OF BUSINESS ORGANIZATION

Franchising 106
Partnership Concept 108
Joint Ventures 109

CHAPTER TEN ORGANIZING AN EFFECTIVE TRAINING PROGRAM

Evaluation of Training Needs 114
Operations Manual as a Vital Training Tool 115
Operator Training Curriculum and Schedule of Classes 125
Ben Franklin Four-Week New-Store-Owner Training Schedule 133

CHAPTER ELEVEN EFFECTIVE PROGRAM IMPLEMENTATION

Operator Supervision by Home Office 144
Supervision via Mutual Assistance 144
Examples of Support Services 147

CHAPTER TWELVE EVALUATING TIMING AND COORDINATION REQUIREMENTS

PERT Technique 152
A Restaurant Company's PERT-CPM 152
PERT-CPM Scheduling 158

CHAPTER ONE
WHAT THE BLUEPRINT DOES

WHAT THE BLUEPRINT DOES

IT PLANS AHEAD   A blueprint, as the term is used throughout this book, is essentially a technique for the planning of a new project. In effect, it helps the planners to think out all aspects of a developmental program on a step-by-step basis.

The blueprint can apply to the evaluation of a complete business or to a particular activity within the business. It can apply to a new start-from-scratch project, something that is completely conceptual, or to an add-on project to be attached to an existing operation.

As a disciplined study, the blueprint process actually forces a company to plan *systematically,* to cover all aspects of a projected activity thoroughly. The blueprint exposes the good and bad points of a program, and, in some instances, it may even show that a proposal should be rejected.

Thus the preparation of a blueprint helps to avoid cluttered thinking and improvisation. It *mandates* that any planned undertaking be carefully thought out in *every* detail; it avoids unexpected "vacuums"—sudden discovery that some areas have not been planned out. It is also interesting how the self-discipline of preparing a detailed plan tends to generate many collateral ideas that lend more and more substance to the original program.

IT ESTIMATES PROSPECTIVE INCOME FACTORS   The blueprint process not only creates operational procedures; it also provides a financial "bottom-line." It can be used to pinpoint all income and expense factors, so that one can enter into a program with detailed knowledge of every potential investment requirement, and all expense and income factors.

Interestingly, the properly prepared blueprint is considered so thoroughly descriptive and so financially credible that in many instances banking circles will make loan commitments on the basis of the financial projections and supporting data it contains. Hence, it serves the dual purpose of a project plan combined with a financial analysis of the plan.

A blueprint also serves the purpose of familiarizing others in the organization with a planned program, thus obtaining valuable feedback and cooperation. As you will note from the Table of Contents, the blueprint covers every possible facet of program development, including a table of organization.

IT ANALYZES   One encounters blueprints mostly in the new business or venture areas of business, where their analytical presentation translates the nebulous to the specific. The usual purpose of becoming specific is to establish the feasibility

IT ANALYZES

of obtaining a profit from the proposed business activity. With consideration of all business factors applicable to the proposal or project, the blueprint should help its users generate a reliable conclusion.

IT STARTS WITH AN IDEA

The whole blueprint process commences with an idea. The idea may have germinated from experience and personal research; the merging of two old ideas to form one new concept; the filling of an apparent marketing vacuum; the transference of basic research into applied research; the marketing promotion of a newly developed product; the creation of an advertising and promotion program for product-introduction; market-share enlargement; or perhaps the practical application of a business hunch. All of these examples have one thing in common: To become effective they must be communicated to other people—people who are decision-makers, be they investors, corporate officers, or venture capitalists. Your blueprint will be the basis of their risk-taking decision.

IT SUBSTANTIATES THE CONCEPT

The blueprint projects the factual parameters within which the basic concept must become operative. It both projects the positive potential and exposes probable dangers. Both are valuable.

The blueprint communicates the ideas of the conceiver, of business associates, of potential investors, and perhaps the banker. Each is able to view, and act on, the bottom-line projection.

The needs a blueprint can fulfill are many and varied. For example, it can help determine the viability of:

- ▶ an acquisition or merger;
- ▶ a new marketing concept;
- ▶ adding a new product, service, or department to the organization;
- ▶ modifying price structure upward or downward.

And it can help the user to determine what personnel are needed to "upgrade" the business effectively.

The blueprint identifies and reveals all of the crucial points of an idea or a planned business, such as:

- ▶ the number of people needed to implement a concept;
- ▶ the amount of capital required;

WHAT THE BLUEPRINT DOES

- the work flow and time duration necessary;
- financing needs;
- profitability projections.

Summed up, the blueprint:

- is the organized planning of a business project;
- achieves effective communication with decision-makers;
- assesses the risk/reward equation;
- projects potential profitability;
- delineates personnel requirements through its Table of Organization;
- establishes a time parameter for accomplishment;
- should assess both feasibility and profitability realistically.

CHAPTER TWO THE NEED

PLAN NOW FOR CHANGE LATER

Today's fast-paced trends point up the necessity for change and diversification in business. It's axiomatic that to forge ahead and grow, business must be constantly progressive and innovative. To remain immobile in an unchanging status is to fall backward—to retrogress.

To cope with our constantly changing environment, the key to success in any business is adaptability. In some cases, adaptability is absolutely necessary for survival. In others, it is the key ingredient for growth and increased profits. Change, then, should be looked upon as an exciting opportunity to enter new fields, to expand, to provide new products or services, to alter the marketing mix, and to forge ahead with new vigor.

The best time to plan for change is when business is good. Should conditions cause a business change before management has considered optional moves, the effect could be a serious setback for the business. Business executives cannot afford complacency.

This is the time for the executive to ask "What if . . . ?" Quick decisions are not called for; there's no need to rush. Instead, a leisurely look ahead and plans for possible change are the order of the day.

SOME CHANGES THAT MIGHT BE ANTICIPATED

CHANGES IN COMPETITIVE MARKETING STRATEGY

Competitive marketing strategy can change quite quickly. What should your business do to counter such changes? Suppose competition suddenly drops prices? Or greatly increases advertising and promotional expenditures? Or changes product in some way which seemingly creates a product advantage? By anticipating such moves, and using program blueprinting to draw up alternative plans, your business can move quickly to counter such competitive activity.

A MAJOR BUYER'S BUSINESS DETERIORATES

Suppose a business is subcontractor to another business which has a big government contract. Although the major buyer's contract is a sizable one—and should require the subcontractor's output for a relatively long period of time—political developments, or changes in the international scene, could suddenly result in the cancellation of business. If the subcontractor has developed alternative customers, or developed other products that could be produced with existing resources and equipment, all is not lost.

SOME CHANGES THAT MIGHT BE ANTICIPATED

NEW COMPETITION MOVES INTO THE NEIGHBORHOOD

What does a retailer of specialty goods do if another store, carrying a similar line, moves into the neighborhood? Have promotional plans been drawn up for such a contingency? Has a new pricing policy been established? Are there plans to broaden the line carried, or for better service to be provided? Should the business move to another location?

LABOR NEEDS CHANGE

A company producing a product that is made with relatively unskilled labor is located near a good source of such labor. But technological developments are creating not only the need for new equipment, but also for more skilled labor. Should this company move? Or retrain its workers? Or attempt to attract skilled labor by advertising? By weighing such options in advance, and by using program blueprinting to determine the most feasible and most cost-advantageous strategy in advance, the company need not lose valuable time in adapting to these new conditions.

CONDITIONS MAY REQUIRE A NEW LOCATION

What does the proprietor of a successful motel do if a new highway draws traffic away from the road on which his business is located? Has he planned for such an event? Does he convert the building to another use or can he sell and rebuild along the new road?

The same situation might be faced by a small, successful retailer in a small but growing town. Is this retailer prepared for the building nearby of a shopping center which could draw customers away?

DO-IT-YOURSELF TREND

Higher prices have resulted in another booming business, the do-it-yourself field. More people are making simple repairs to their cars and auto supply outlets have never been busier. Homeowners are doing their own remodeling and repairs. The result: a tremendous increase in the demand for do-it-yourself tools. With this demand has come the concomitant demand for do-it-yourself books.

LEISURE TREND

American consumers have revised their priorities. Despite the do-it-yourself trend, the money saved is not all going into the bank. People are enjoying leisure time more than ever. Sporting goods, casual clothes, cameras, outdoor vehicles, camping equipment, swimming pools, and yard furniture are just a few examples of product lines that are in greater demand than ever because of the expanding leisure-time market.

NEW POPULATION TRENDS

It used to be said that the management was concerned with "men, money, machines, and material." However, more women are employed outside their homes than ever before. More couples are delaying the birth of their first child. The birth rate is down and families are smaller. The population of the United States is growing older progressively. How does this affect the strategy of a company marketing baby products? Or the firm designing women's clothes? An awareness of change —and the ability to adapt to it—is a critical function of corporate management.

In anticipating change, many new ideas can be developed which utilize existing resources or which require only minimal investment in new personnel and facilities. A retail chain may consider "adding on" a mail-order department. A manufacturer might consider the leasing of its product, or servicing it directly. A publisher may see great potential in developing a new division which would market specialized books, through new channels.

These new endeavors must pay their own way; they must also return an acceptable level of profit. Businesses can no longer afford the luxury of carrying products or services which do not provide a reasonable return on investment. Cost accounting should accurately assign overhead and direct costs to all operating units. In today's competitive environment every department, each division, and every outlet must be considered as a separate profit center.

NEW IDEAS—SPECIALIZATION

Finally, the entrepreneur may have an idea whose time has not yet come. The market may not be there—yet. Technology may not be sufficiently advanced, but inevitably it will be. The business may have to await developments in the market or in other businesses. Whatever the reason, looking ahead and weighing future options and courses of action is sound practice. Ideas can be discussed. Preliminary plans can be prepared and cost factors can be weighed. When the time is right, sound planning can provide the necessary advantage over competitors and the resources to implement the project successfully.

Also, the need to compete on a price basis has produced a host of enterprises which specialize in products and services that other businesses used to provide. Today, a car-owner who needs a new muffler or work on a transmission can take his or her car to a company specializing in one of those functions. By specializing, these outlets can stock a larger product and parts inventory and provide faster service. Since employees provide only one service, minimal skill is required and training is greatly simplified.

DEVELOPING OPTIONS

These are just some of the developments which could affect a thriving business. By acknowledging that such developments are possible, even probable, the business can consider alternative options. Management may study cost factors, look into what is involved in changing location, draw up possible changes in organizational structure, consider the legal ramifications, and be prepared to move in response to changing circumstances. Careful advance planning enables the business to progress.

AVAILABILITY OF NEW MARKETS

While changes in the marketplace can be frustrating, they should be looked upon as exciting opportunities to enter new fields, to expand, to provide new products or services, to alter the marketing mix, and to forge ahead. To the relatively new enterprise, these activities can be exciting and challenging.

Any expanding business, in order to choose among its options, must have information. Accurate, reliable information has never been in such demand by business as it is today. Large corporations have entire departments devoted to collecting information and organizing it in formats which company executives can use in the decision-making process. Often this involves sophisticated, computerized operations. Research specialists occupy a position high on corporate organization charts. Economists, too, have become more evident in corporate structures. Providing information for the use of others has become big business.

Many smaller businesses, of course, cannot afford the luxury of such information systems. But the information is there, if one knows where to look for it. Every good small business executive keeps abreast of developments in the field through the reading of trade journals and contacts with those with whom the business deals. Membership in the local Chamber of Commerce is helpful. However, there are many other information sources. These include seminars and research libraries and data banks. Subscription to business reports of all kinds is also constructive. And small computers are now being sold at reasonable prices—or they may be leased. Government agencies are good sources of information and much of their information is either free or obtainable at minimum cost. Finally, an outside consultant can be employed on a per-diem basis.

NEED TO ASSESS CURRENT TRENDS

The potential business opportunity can take many forms. The business entrepreneur may see a need for a product that does not exist, or for a service not being provided. It's a new era, a different market. Before proceeding with development, many factors must be considered. Is additional research required? A manufacturer must consider the cost of design. Must new machinery be purchased or a plant expanded? What are the material requirements, where shall they be obtained, and what will the costs be? Is the business talent to market the new product available within the organization, or must additional specialized personnel be hired? Finally, can the new product be marketed at a price which is compatible with anticipated demand and which will yield an acceptable profit?

INNOVATION, DIVERSIFICATION, AND ADD-ON PROFIT CENTERS

It's imperative that business recognize and respond to the continuous shifting of consumer receptivity and other business changes. Change is constant; what was suitable and adequate yesterday may be inappropriate today. There is a constant need to recognize and respond to changes—to innovate, to diversify, to add new products and services so that sales potential may be enlarged and the corporate image refurbished.

INNOVATION

Innovation is recognized by most businesses as a basic requirement for success. It is reflected in constant changes in decor, products, locations, services, promotions—in fact, in practically every aspect of a business. To keep abreast of changes, successful businesses maintain expensive research and development departments and conduct continuous field surveys among both consumers and dealers. Businesses today recognize the need for innovation and seek to gain the initiative before their competitors.

One common and effective innovation is the "catalog corner." This is a designated corner or area within an existing business that another company rents or leases to make its catalog and order forms (and usually an employee to take catalog orders) available to the public. A major department store/mail-order house recently introduced "catalog corners" in drug stores and other appropriate locations. These "corners" acted to multiply the available sales and profit centers while avoiding many of the normal operating costs.

Another common innovation is to change the product-line mix. This frequently increases profitability for a business at a minimal increase in operating expense. For example, in the fast-food field several of the giants have substantially expanded their menu mix to increase customer traffic, sales, and earnings. In addition to the standard specialties with which they started, many now offer salad bars, sundaes, and various other foods. Also, recent breakfast add-ons have smoothed traffic curves and created new profit centers merely by more intensive use of the same overhead.

DIVERSIFICATION

Diversification is required not only to offset rising overhead but also to keep pace with competition, protect markets by recognizing changes in consumer buying attitudes, and introduce additional profit centers which will produce income by more intensive utilization of overhead. Drug stores are perhaps the most common and long-standing example of this, having long since included everything from lunch counters to hardware departments with their prescription centers. Supermarkets, in some places, include such disparate enterprises as bakery outlets and flower shops. And some major department store chains now also operate auto service centers and restaurants.

ADD-ON PROFIT CENTERS

Some businesses seek to increase profits by operating secondary, company-owned businesses. During the past several years some gas stations, for example, have acquired new profit-center businesses to occupy available bays or, in some cases, the complete station. Such businesses include auto parts sales shops, doughnut shops, convenience food stores, etc. Conversely, some convenience food stores now also sell gasoline.

There are many other examples, but the key to all of these separate profit-center ideas is to use existing overhead more efficiently and more intensively. In this way a minimum of working capital is involved in the increase of profit-making potential.

CHAPTER THREE
THE PROCESS OF BLUEPRINT PREPARATION

PREPARATORY STEPS

ESTABLISHING A RATIONALE

The blueprint is typically prepared sequentially, in a step-by-step fashion. Initially, it is necessary to evaluate the planned program's feasibility—to establish its rationale. This feasibility evaluation represents, in effect, a preliminary "balance sheet" that compares the program's positive and negative aspects and helps management to determine whether the program merits further consideration.

DESCRIBING THE PROJECT

The blueprint should contain a clear statement of the program and its objectives. This statement should be accompanied by an analysis of each business factor that could have any possible bearing on the basic concept or concepts upon which the program is built.

The advantages of the project should be defined precisely. The blueprint is a document, and its purpose is to communicate an idea. The manner in which it is organized, written, and presented should catch and hold the attention of the reader and accurately convey the merits of the idea.

ESTABLISHING PRIOR GOALS

In large part, project feasibility often depends on management's statement of its goals before the studies that form the blueprint are initiated. In most instances management will have already defined the basic policies within which the company will function. (And this should *always* be the case with programs that are to be developed within the framework of an existing, functioning business entity.) Further, these policies will be subject to modification as management responds to changes in market and other conditions and communicates these modifications to the organization. Thus, evaluating feasibility is a continuous process—one that is dynamic, rather than static.

It is always desirable to have established project policy, criteria, and goals prior to any short-term and/or long-term feasibility evaluation. A proper evaluation will indicate probable project results, an accomplishment that is useful in its own right. But it is far more useful (and in some cases vitally necessary) that probable results be weighed against objectively stated requirements. As an example, a specific company may contemplate embarking on a project that exhibits a projected probable return on investment of 30 percent—but the company's management will be influenced more by comparing that projected return with current corporate return requirements.

An unrealistic investment return in this instance of, say, 35 percent could mitigate against beginning the project or contemplating it further.

Here are some areas that require continuing evaluation, the results of which must be communicated to middle management in order that it function efficiently:

1. Policy
2. Performance criteria
3. Goal establishment
   a) Short-term
   b) Long-term
4. Profitability
5. Budget establishment
6. Budget performance
7. Market share
8. Competition's position with respect to
   a) Share-of-market
   b) Innovation
   c) Image
   d) Profitability
   e) Product distribution
9. Management performance

STRUCTURING THE PROJECT

A blueprint that is comprehensive and that leads to valid decisions concerning project embarkation and implementation should address all relevant subjects, including:

1. *Feasibility:* Have all envisioned positive and negative factors been listed and compared? Has the prospective market for the program's product and/or service been evaluated?

2. *Arithmetic:* Have the income and expenses been projected and evaluated? Have potential earnings over a period of from three to five years been assessed?

3. *Image:* What appearance will the final product have? Will considerations of image projection be a determinate in site selection, structure construction, and other areas?

THE PROCESS OF BLUEPRINT PREPARATION

4. *Finance:* What financing is available for the project; and of what type is it?

5. *Implementation:* How should the project be developed and implemented; and who should be responsible for development and implementation?

6. *Format:* What business format best suits the project? Should the venture be organized as a proprietorship, a partnership, a corporation, a joint venture, or perhaps some other form of business organization?

7. *Legal requirements:* What types of legal services will be required to develop and to implement the program? Are licenses, permits, and other governmental approvals necessary?

8. *Personnel requirements:* What types of persons are required to develop and implement the program? What qualifications should each of them possess and has a table of organization been drawn to depict reporting and functional responsibilities. How and at what rate should their work be compensated?

9. *Advertising and promotion:* What advertising budget should be established, on what should it be based, and how should it be expended? Are promotions necessary to attract customer flow and, if so, what should they be?

10. *Support:* Is continuing support and backup required to ensure the program's success? Have support and backup services been defined accurately, together with a realistic projection of the cost of each?

11. *Training:* Is formal and/or informal training required to orient participants thoroughly in all aspects of the program? Over how long a period of time should training take place, and what is the projected cost of training?

12. *Production:* Are present production facilities adequate to cope with a sudden upsurge in demand? If not, can alternate production and/or supply arrangements be made within the bounds of economic viability?

ONE COMPANY'S PRELIMINARY STEPS

One company, in blueprinting its contemplated corporate expansion, listed the following items or information as being necessary for the preparation of its blueprint and the implementation of its program:

PREPARATORY STEPS

1. Management's statement of objectives;
2. Sales projections for each product and service;
3. Complete cost information;
4. A thorough description of the channels of distribution that the company would utilize to deliver its products and services to the consumer;
5. Projected profit-and-loss projections for a five-year period;
6. Projected cash flow for a three-year period;
7. A forecast of income and expense by defined growth phase, as differentiated from time period;
8. An organization chart for each defined growth phase;
9. A manpower plan;
10. A schedule of hiring;
11. Job descriptions for all key personnel;
12. A determination of capital investment required to develop and implement the program.
13. Definition of the company's capital funding sources and a capital funding structure;
14. A sequence of events schedule for program implementation in PERT/CPM form;
15. Operating manuals;
16. Organization, definition, and curricula for required training programs.

PRIOR RESEARCH REQUIRED

Among the many items of information required to develop data for the preparation of a blueprint is a determination of the market for the company's product and/or services. Since the value of the completely developed blueprint is directly related to the reliability of this determination, it is important to conduct all necessary basic research. Market projections are key to the total plan, and the size and scope of the company's goals—and its plans for attaining them—are developed from these projections. The need for manpower to staff the organization; expenditures that will be required for product and facilities; and advertising, sales, and promotional plans are all directly related to and dependent on the share of the market that the company hopes to obtain.

The importance of accumulating, analyzing, and synthesizing basic market data cannot be overstressed. The success of the overall program depends in major part on the quality of the blueprint—but the quality of the blueprint is almost totally dependent on the reliability of marketing projections. This reliability, in its turn, depends on the depth of the study that generated the basic data from which the projections were developed. A number of other factors are also considered, such as research budget, time allowed for completion of the research, the availability of talented personnel to generate and process the data—and even the form in which necessary data exist; whether they may be obtained from readily available statistical data banks or must be obtained by arduous field work.

Frequently, a budget determines the scope and depth of market research. In developing this budget it is imperative to recognize that a prediction of attaining the plan's goals is only as reliable as the marketing data upon which the plan is based.

EVALUATING FEASIBILITY

BUSINESS FEASIBILITY CRITERIA In blueprinting any new business or the expansion of an existing business, the basic viability of the planned venture should be considered carefully. The following 16-point feasibility criteria consists of questions that have been found to be helpful in determining basic viability:

1. Do you have sufficient qualified personnel in your organization to effectively handle the commitments of the proposed new program?

2. Do you have adequate financial capabilities? Never attempt to enter a new enterprise if you are under-capitalized or "running scared" financially. Under these circumstances, your business is generally destined to fail.

3. Have you researched the market? Is there justifiable "positioning" for the planned new business in the market? Can you project adequate sales and earnings for it?

4. Is the planned new product or service distinctive? How and why is it better than related products? Does it have enduring customer appeal? Distinctiveness can take many forms, such as packaging,

merchandising, servicing, and structural format. Does your product or service offer something different, something that is not offered by competitive products or services?

5. Is the profit margin adequate? Make sure that the business can, realistically, deliver a desirable net profit in minimum time. Many businesses recapture their initial capitalization within three years.

6. Is the product or service trainable? Can a person with little or no experience be taught how to operate the business successfully?

7. Does the product or service exhibit a repeat factor? According to the "oil for the lamps of China" theory, lamps are distributed free in order to generate repeat oil business. The "razor, razor blade" concept stresses the same fundamental principle. Such repeat-patronage elements in a product or service tend to create an "annuity" type of business, as compared to the single-sale business.

8. Can your product or service be projected into a national market or has it only regional acceptance? If it enjoys a national market, do you have sufficient resources to supply outlets efficiently and economically in any part of the country?

9. Does your product require installation? If so, can installation be farmed out to local tradesmen or technicians? Can installation be accomplished at a reasonable, predetermined price?

10. Are freight costs an important element in the sale of your product? Must you ship heavy or bulky products? Will excessive freight charges reduce profits? Will regional warehousing solve the problem? Or would minimum full-carload area shipments be preferable?

11. Do you have sufficient unutilized production capacity to meet a sharp increase in sales? You can be ruined by unforeseen success. A classic example was a franchisor operating in the industrial infrared heating field. Initial sales were better than expectations; the first trainee group produced over one million sales in a short period of time. The business was not able to produce this volume, was unable to subcontract, and the expected acquisition of a larger factory failed to materialize. The result was failure due to success.

12. What is the depth of your personnel? Do you have sufficient personnel with the ability to administer your program, or is your pres-

ent staff occupied with the normal, day-to-day workload of your present business? If the latter is the case, you must expand your staff to meet new program requirements.

13. Do you have a viable financing plan? In most business operations, financing is generally required for land, structure, equipment, inventory, and modernization. Financing is ordinarily accomplished by use of funds obtained from one or more of the following sources:
    a) The company, which finances the structure, lease, or inventory.
    b) The lessor, who, in many instances, will subordinate land and/or build to suit, taking a prescribed percentage or rental as compensation. Builders and contractors will also build to suit on the same terms.
    c) Local banks, who may know the company and its success potential based on a previous venture.
    d) Governmental lending sources (such as the SBA, FHA, and HUD), whose loans have been minimal recently but may become available more easily in the future.
    e) Lease insurance, which guarantees a lease for its entire term, thereby relieving the company of a substantial contingent liability. This type of lease insurance is available through a number of SBA-associated firms.
    f) Private investment sources (including SBIC's insurance companies, private investors, and private syndicates) which can provide both debt and equity capital. Syndicates frequently consist of professional groups—such as physicians, dentists, and accountants—who are receptive to absentee ownership and, possibly, certain tax advantages. Syndicates have financed motels, nursing homes, and other large investment franchises and other businesses.
    g) Minority group financing sources (such as the MESBIC program), which involve private investors operating in special programs sponsored by the federal government.

14. What is the growth position of your industry? What percentage of your market has been saturated? Is your industry's annual compounded growth rate increasing progressively, or is your industry mature and showing signs of decline? Naturally, an industry with

minimum past-market exploitation and an excellent expansion potential is a more desirable environment for a venture.

15. Can you maintain your competitive position? You may be strong in your regional market but can you be equally strong in another market area which may already be dominated by a national operator? Can you compete there? How will you go about it?

16. Are your profit projections realistic? What is your present share of the market? Do you have sufficient capital and managerial competence to expand your share of the market with the same profit margins you have enjoyed in the past, or will you have to price-cut to enter the new market? Are your growth rates sound? Has your present operation demonstrated that your growth projections are within the realm of possible achievement?

FEASIBILITY EVALUATION: EXAMPLE 1:

A theoretical manufacturer of cutting instruments used by meat-markets and related businesses, Mason Blades Company, is considering the feasibility of replacing its present channels of distribution with a system of franchised distributors. The company's management has retained an outside firm of independent consultants to prepare a feasibility report on this subject, and this report follows as Exhibit 3.1.

Exhibit 3.1 Mason Blades Company Feasibility Report

Our preliminary evaluations concerning the feasibility of Mason Blades Company's developing a franchised system for the purpose of distributing its products are developed in the following pages. The following list of 15 topics and the questions to which each topic leads represents the prime criteria that served as standards of measurement:

1. *Quality of the product:* Are the Mason blades and other products equal or superior to other similar products available today? What available documentation can support product claims? Were quality evaluation tests scientifically conducted in laboratories as well as in the field? What is the scope of customer acceptance of these tests?

2. *Parent company experience and support:* Is Mason Blades Company capable of developing and supporting a franchise organization? Can it provide the investment in personnel and capital to expand through franchising? Is the present management team qualified to nurture the "embryo" franchisees?

THE PROCESS OF BLUEPRINT PREPARATION

3. *Production capacity:* Are present production facilities capable of meeting the increased demands of a rapidly expanding franchise network? Can Mason Blades give reasonable assurance that it can deliver promptly all over the country, even internationally, with present production capacities? How quickly can it increase its production?

4. *The market:* Is the present and future market for meat blades large enough to justify a considerable investment for expanded operations? Can Mason Blades anticipate capturing a significantly larger share of this market from its competitors? What effect will the expanded Mason Blades operations have on present distributors?

5. *Merchandising:* Does Mason Blades have the kind of effective, coordinated merchandising program required to compete in today's active, changing market? Is there a distinctive, uniform packaging plan? Has a strong and distinctive brand image been developed?

6. *Prices and profit margins:* Are Mason Blades' products competitively priced? Is there a need for competitive pricing? Do present manufacturer profit margins allow for increased expenditures in many areas, such as national advertising, costlier packaging, and franchise development investment?

7. *Advertising and promotion:* Does Mason Blades have, or plan, a national advertising program to develop consumer acceptance of their product? Are present catalogs effective? What materials have they provided for their distributors to stimulate sales? Have they developed a lead-time procurement system?

8. *Company image:* Can Mason Blades build a distinctive company image for itself and for its products? Is it readily recognized as a prime industry factor? Where does it stand in relation to competitors?
   ▶ *Unique appeal:* One of the important necessities for most franchise programs is a distinctive, outstanding concept that positions the company in its field and that can be exploited successfully for the mutual benefit of the franchisee and the franchisor. Is this present, or can it be developed?

9. *Present distribution:* Will the established system of nationwide distributors interfere in any way with the development of a franchise program? Will franchisees tend to have a disruptive influence on

these outlets? What guarantees of exclusivity will the franchisees require? What assurance of territorial integrity can they be given?

10. *Methodology:* Has the company evolved methods and techniques that could be adapted to the projected franchise? Are there any computerized systems that can be extended to the franchisees in any way? Has the company "manualized" any procedures? Is there a codified set of policies that can be applied or adapted to the franchise network?

11. *Teaching systems:* Are any unusual difficulties anticipated in developing training programs? Are all necessary skills and techniques capable of being analyzed, organized, and incorporated into a formal course of instruction? Can this course of instruction be structured in a condensed form and taught in a short time? What field training will be required?

12. *Prototype operations:* Is there an existing operation with which the franchisee can identify? Can the franchisee see himself or herself as the owner of an existing, profitable business? Does this business now operate in a manner that is identical or closely related to the projected franchise? To what entity can the franchise salesperson point with pride? Is there a shining example of success?

13. *Franchisee assurance:* Can Mason Blades offer a prospective franchisee reasonable assurance of achieving an improved opportunity for financial gain? Will an opportunity to build equity in the business be available? Is the inventory valuable and stable?

14. *Investment and profits:* Can the franchise produce significant earnings with relative ease? Will profits justify investment of money and effort? Will the franchisee's earnings increase steadily?

15. *Prospective franchisees:* What are the prospects for franchising today and in the future? What capital is available for investment? What is the tenor of the franchise industry? What are the chances of selling this proposed franchise?

Although many additional criteria might be considered, these are sufficient to enable us to make a valid judgment of the feasibility of the Mason Blades concept. Considering them also indicates areas in which changes, improvements, and innovations are required to improve the prospects of the venture.

THE PROCESS OF BLUEPRINT PREPARATION

evaluation
Our evaluation is that the Mason Blade Company could anticipate achieving substantial earnings from the development of a franchised distributor network, and that the investment required and the risks involved are significantly outweighed by the profit potential.

product quality
Our studies of the company and inquiries in the field substantiated all claims made by Mason Blades for the superior quality of its products and the growing number of well-satisfied users. Indeed, it is possible that the company has understated claims of superiority, durability, and efficiency for its present hard-edge blades. Many customers indicate that they are able to use blades far longer than company recommendations. Introduction of newer, more durable blades, which will form the keystone of the franchise program, could result in even more spectacular customer satisfaction. Documentation of these experiences should be started immediately, as well as verification of all scientific laboratory and field-test data. A collection of approvals and compliments should be built in the form of testimonials, letters, and laboratory reports for use by all company sales agents.

company management
The leadership demonstrated by the management of Mason Blades Company has convinced us of its capability to establish and support a franchise system. Mason Blades' growth over the years, in an orderly and profitable pattern, testifies to this. Management's willingness to adapt to the most modern systems and equipment further indicates its awareness of current and future trends. Mason Blades has continually taken steps to lead its industry in testing and using workable innovations. Management has undertaken deep analytical studies of Mason Blades Company in an effort to make a judgment regarding the future course of company expansion. Its wholehearted commitment to the concept of controlled company growth and development of a structure to support such growth leads us to conclude that the company and its executives will be equally dedicated to the guidance of each franchisee as they embark upon a program of franchised expansion.

product line expansion
Plans for expanding present saw, knife, and plate manufacturing facilities are formulated and we understand that the production capacity of Mason Blades can be doubled as soon as there is a signal need. This will allow management to meet a sharp upward surge in demand as franchises are sold. Currently, however, the company should explore the reasons for delayed deliveries to

dealers and distributors that we observed, and immediately institute procedures to speed deliveries.

the market
The current market for disposable hard-edge saws, knives, and plates is estimated to be between eight and ten million dollars a year. We estimate that it can grow to several times this size during the next five years. This factor alone is sufficient to justify a very significant investment for operational expansion. It is highly probable that Mason Blades can obtain an increasingly larger share of this rapidly growing market by clearly taking the lead in structuring newer and more efficient distribution systems.

market potential
An aggressive franchise system selling Mason Blade's superior disposable hard-edge products can demonstrate the value of the "throw-away" system and effect a gradually deepening penetration into the resharpenable saw service market. In our opinion, all rental services can be affected, including competitors.

price structure
Mason Blades Company's resale and distributor price structure is still significantly lower than that of its principal competitors. In our opinion, as the new hard-edge products are introduced, a higher price range can be established, to provide greater revenue to finance more imaginative packaging, more advertising and promotional support, and a completely integrated franchise program. However, the present discount structure should remain the same in order to provide adequate profit margins and incentives needed for franchising.

advertising and promotion
A truly creative and carefully constructed advertising and promotion campaign, coupled with an improved merchandising plan, could quickly help Mason Blades establish its own identity in the industry. It's necessary to work to build a new, imaginative, and distinctive brand image that will immediately convey all the features of Mason Blade's products—quality control and manufacturing capabilities, durability, superiority, reliability, efficiency, and technological advancement. As the company develops a greater share of the market, it will assume a more distinctive presence in the mind of the customer and the competition. The materials developed to aid franchisees, plus an expanding advertising campaign, will accrue to the benefit of all distributors of Mason Blades, franchised and nonexclusive.

franchisee appeal

The unique appeal of Mason Blades Company's products can be seen in their demonstrated present and potential future superiority. This can be shown effectively to prospective franchisees as one of the "keys" leading to a profitable exclusive distributorship. Further proof of the validity of this appeal will be documented from company records and augmented as soon as additional substantiation is developed from current and future field operations.

franchise establishment strategy

At the outset of the franchise development program, it is suggested that franchises be established in those areas where present distribution is weakest, provided, of course, that market area studies indicate that a specifically located franchisee can succeed. As the franchise program develops, operating experiences gained from the franchisees will point the way toward development of better merchandising programs, which can be utilized for the benefit of the entire distribution system. Mason Blades will have to provide each franchisee with some assurance of a territory that generally excludes existing Mason Blades distributors. Present distributors could be offered an opportunity to purchase a franchise for their own operating area. The strongest distributor in each area should be given preference. Where a distributor fails to become an exclusive franchisee, the company should seek to sell a franchise for that area and discontinue all other distributors in the particular territory.

The relative performance of a franchisee or a nonexclusive distributor in a specific area is easily determinable and it is anticipated that Mason Blade's management will have no difficulties in making value judgments. The franchise development program can replace weak distributors with strong franchisees. It can result in a smaller, more productive, more easily directed sales organization.

franchisee training

Mason Blades Company's franchise training program can be structured along conventional franchise training lines. There are no exceptional skills required on the part of the franchisee. Basically, the franchisee should have good sales aptitudes and some sales experience. The trainer should be capable of motivating the franchisee and heightening the enthusiasm which will have been aroused by the franchise salesman.

prototype

To prove much of the opinion, belief, and theory stated here, it is urgent that Mason Blades Company establish one or two prototype operations which will, in every respect and appearance, be identical with the franchised business offering. A "manualized" operating system and procedures must be created. A prototype franchisee must be trained. A tested advertising and promotion campaign, as well as every other tool and device helpful in ensuring success should be provided. To assure franchisee success, an unusual amount of support in many areas, physical as well as financial, should be offered wherever possible, with regional advertising to support the franchisee. The operator will require systems for inventory and expense control. Most important, a satisfactory growth and success pattern should be developed which can be used to demonstrate to prospects how they can also prosper with a Mason Blades Company franchise.

franchisee assurance

When one or two successful prototypes have been established a prospective franchisee will have reasonable assurance that it is possible to succeed equally as well as the prototype business. The franchise will have the advantage of prototype experience, which the prototype did not have, plus the impetus of company growth. This advantage coupled with the efforts of the prototypes and the other franchisees, plus the expanded efforts of the company, will create a geometric progression toward greater achievement for all.

franchisee investment

The franchisee's investment will be small in comparison to earnings. It will be possible to earn three to five times the required investment the first year of business. The nature of the business is such that reorders generally will be automatic and the franchisee will be able to devote most of his or her effort to opening new accounts, thereby assuring a continually increasing flow of orders and profits. For the trained person, the business itself is easy. Observations of successful Mason Blade distributors indicate that the franchisee should be able to close a very high percentage of leads.

FEASIBILITY EVALUATION: EXAMPLE 2

A theoretical wholesale druggist decides to explore the feasibility of studying the use of the franchise method of marketing and distribution in its own operations. In contrast to Mason Blades Company's basic question of whether franchising is feasible for its operation, the wholesale druggist asks a much more simple question: "Is it worthwhile for me to *consider* franchising?" To answer this question—and determine whether it's worthwhile to study franchising in more detail in relation to its own operations—the druggist must develop answers to two basic and subsidiary questions:

1. What benefits can be offered to *prospective* franchisees that will entice them to become *actual* franchisees?

2. What benefits can accrue to the wholesale druggist from a network of franchised retailers?

These listings of relative benefits, the weight of which indicates the feasibility of considering franchising as a method of marketing and distribution, follows as Exhibit 3.2.

Exhibit 3.2 basic franchisee benefits
Wholesale Druggist Feasibility Evaluation

1. The exclusive right to do business within a specified territory.
   a) The right and obligation to use the parent company's identity.
   b) The right to use the parent company's methods, procedures, business secrets, and copyrighted promotional materials and operating manuals.

2. The assistance of the parent company with respect to site selection, lease negotiations, store layout, and design.

3. Initial training.
   a) Training at the parent company's home offices, with the curriculum designed to indoctrinate the operator in the techniques of a successful operation.
   b) Field training at the operator's retail store, consisting of an on-the-job application to daily operations of the techniques learned at the parent company's home offices, under the supervision and with the assistance of a qualified representative of the parent company.

4. Continuing training and assistance programs.
   a) Periodic visits from the Operations Manager.
   b) Unlimited telephone and mail consultation.
   c) Refresher courses in new methods of merchandising, peripheral and profitable operations, and promotions.
   d) Periodic regional meetings and seminars.
   e) Newsletters.

5. Continuing promotion programs.
   a) Point-of-sale displays for new items and ideas.
   b) Newspaper advertising mats.
   c) Publicity releases.
   d) Themes for seasonal display decors.
   e) Window displays.

6. Business advisory services.
   a) Consultation on promotional, business, or operating problems.
   b) Analysis of monthly and yearly operating results.

basic franchisor benefits

1. The system's rate of expansion can be controlled. By adjusting various segments of the company's overall budget, the rate of acquiring new operators can be increased or decreased as desired.

2. The franchisor's activities are financed by the operator. Following the sale of a relatively few territories, the program becomes self-sustaining and initial investment is liquidated.

3. Expansion of the franchised network will create greater franchisor purchasing power—which should lead to increased discounts and efficiencies.

4. Peripheral operating profit can be realized with a franchised operation in the areas of advertising, sale of furniture and fixtures to operators, sale of equipment to operators and the capital gains realized from selling these items at a profit from company-owned stores.

5. Uniform training and merchandising procedures will generally improve overall operations, including those owned by the parent company.

PREPARATION OF A BLUEPRINT'S TABLE OF CONTENTS

The areas that are normally analyzed and interrelated within a Blueprint are typified by the sample Table of Contents that follows as Exhibit 3.3.

Exhibit 3.3 Blueprint Table of Contents

Subject	Section
Description of concept	1
Market analysis	2
Markets by rank	3
Market potential	4
Marketing stages	5
Size of the market	6
Probable trading area	7
Market share	8

(cont.)

THE PROCESS OF BLUEPRINT PREPARATION

Subject	Section
Consumer surveys	9
Survey questionnaires	10
Distribution of interviews	11
Tabulation of questionnaires	12
Market survey conclusions	13
Site location criteria	14
Corporate identification by: logo; trademark; building design	15
Trademark registration	16
Table of organization	17
Job descriptions	18
Personnnel standards: executive; general administrative; labor;	19
Personnel training programs	20
Personnel phasing	21
Publicity and public relations	22
Advertising	23
Community participation	24
Description of plant and equipment	25
Plant capacity	26
Operations manual	27
Break-even analysis	28
Capital investment required	29
Projected return on capital	30
PERT/CPM: Project Evaluation and Review Technique/Critical Path Method Charts	31

CHAPTER FOUR

PROGRAM ARITHMETIC: EXAMINING THE BOTTOM LINE

THE ARITHMETIC OF BUSINESS—THE BOTTOM LINE

THE BASIS OF BUSINESS DECISIONS

Before embarking on a new venture or project, a company must be assured not only that the endeavor will pay its own way, but that it will be a source of income. The company will not entertain a project that does not exhibit an excellent potential for producing an appropriate return on investment, or ROI. And the amount of profit must be satisfactory when considered in light of the resources that must be committed by the company. The projected bottom line is the basis for management decisions. It cannot be otherwise.

THE BASIS OF THE BOTTOM LINE

Market data are the basis of all financial and marketing projections. Realistic projections fully consider at least the following factors:

- Product manufacturing costs
- Factory sales prices
- Distributor sales prices
- Consumer sales prices
- Potential sales volume
- Probable sales volume
- Variable expenses
- Fixed expenses
- Budgets
- Controls
- Sources of income
- Sources of capital
- Required investment

Realistic projections also consist of a minimum of the following projected statements:

- Income statements
- Cash flows
- Break-even analyses.

In many instances, projected balance sheets and other projections and analyses are required, as well.

THE ARITHMETIC OF BUSINESS – THE BOTTOM LINE

THE BASIC PROJECTIONS

As pragmatic dollars-and cents data are developed and utilized to perform projections and analyses, feasibility unfolds, and management is able to make a wide variety of decisions. The relationship between cost and sales price determines potential profit for each segment of the channel of distribution. This relationship also determines the effectiveness of how and how many company products or services reach the market and ultimately the consumer. *Break-even charts* depict the dynamic relationship of profit and loss to sales volume, graphically representing their interlinked nature. *Cash flow projections* provide management with information concerning the cash inflows and cash outflows of the business, and of the business' resulting fluctuations in cash position over selected periods of time. The most important results are those which reflect projected peak cash outflows and net profit before and after taxes.

ASSESSMENT OF INCOME AND EXPENSE FACTORS

The arithmetic of a program consists of a number of projections. Essentially, and subject to qualifications that will be stated later, these projections concern themselves with the program's income and expense factors, and with its cash-in and cash-out factors. In the former case, the projection is commonly called a "pro-forma income statement," and in the latter case it is commonly called a "pro-forma cash flow." Although the two projections are quite similar in format, they should not be confused. As will be explained in greater detail, it is usually wise to ascertain potential profitability first by examining the pro-forma income statement, and then to ascertain probable capital requirements by examining the pro-forma cash flow.

THE PROJECTIONS' OBJECTIVES

All projections are assumptive. During the preliminary or conceptual stages of developing a new program and the blueprint for that program, they are *purely* assumptive. Nonetheless, they are not only important—they are critical. Their purpose is to provide a preliminary financial definition of the various stages through which the program will go during its implementation. Their objectives are to define estimates of the program's cost at each stage, to define estimates of the income which should be realized during each stage, and to provide clear statements of the program's financial goals.

THE PROJECTIONS' VALUES

During the process of program implementation, the last of these objectives is of primary importance. As the program is implemented, the arithmetic portion of the blueprint will function as a financial operating plan against which actual performance may be compared at specific intervals and/or at the occurrence of specified events. Deviations from the blueprint's projected performance will be a major determinant of management's decisions concerning continuation or abandonment of the program, the devotion of greater or lesser effort to it, and whether the blueprint itself should be modified.

Prior to implementation of the program, however, the projections that form the blueprint's arithmetic section are of even greater importance, and that importance is multifaceted:

1. The preparation of these projections forces the disciplined statement of the diverse factors of which the total program consists. Many otherwise well-conceived programs fail because their creators have overlooked key factors. The probability of committing this error is reduced drastically by the simple process of writing key assumptions on a piece of paper—a step that is necessary in the preparation of any projection.

2. The person preparing the projections tends to acquire a feeling for the financial aspects of the program. In addition, upon examining the projections, others involved with the project will find that their knowledge of the interrelationships that exist among the program's various aspects has been increased significantly. On more than one occasion, the person preparing the projections has noted an expense or income item become increasingly more important to the program's overall success. The pattern of numbers attached to that one item or group of items led to a further extensive and very detailed analysis of the assumptions that led to the pattern—in some cases, additional research was conducted to affirm or deny the validity of key ingredients. Sometimes a flaw was uncovered and the entire program was abandoned—and a logically consequent major loss was avoided. In other instances, assumptions were found to be soundly or conservatively based and the project proceeded—but with more confidence on the part of everyone involved in its conception and implementation.

3. There is, for some reason, a traditional conflict between people responsible for finance and those responsible for marketing. Financial personnel tend toward conservativism and minimization of budgets, operating

in the main in accordance with the very sound philosophy that the less money a company spends, the greater its profit will be. Marketing personnel, on the other hand, tend to be somewhat more aggressive, and usually seek increased advertising budgets, increased salaries and/or commissions for salesmen, and the like. They operate in accordance with the equally sound philosophy that increased budgets in the area of marketing will lead to increased sales, and the more money a company makes, the greater its profit will be.

Examination of the projections for a program—preferably during the course of, or immediately followed by, a meeting of all personnel responsible for critical areas of the program's implementation—serves to increase the understanding of the overall program by those responsible for individual functional areas. Financial personnel are made more aware of the importance of marketing and generating sales; marketing personnel are made more aware of the critical nature of cost control and budget limitations; production personnel can see clearly the impact of their decisions concerning inventory levels on marketing and finance; and so it goes through every aspect of the planned program. Communication among various key personnel is often increased—a goal which should be sought in the development and implementation of any program.

4. Properly noted, the set of projections can, and often does, form an integral part of attracting investors to the program, in those cases where this is felt to be necessary or wise. Their very existence, as well as their content, tends to convey the impression to potential investors —whether they be sources of loans such as banks, or sources of equity capital such as potential partners, or even sources of credit such as suppliers—that the people with whom they are dealing are reasonable, responsible businesspeople with a well-thought-out, sound program. In light of the fact that potential investors generally have a number of investment alternatives readily available to them, their cooperation is enormously important. And that cooperation may reasonably be expected to increase as a result of their examination of thoughtfully conceived projections.

It must be stressed, however, that *the quality of the assumptions utilized in developing any pro-forma statement is the primary determinant of that pro-forma statement's usefulness.* If one has great confidence—based on careful research, thought, and experience—in the assumptions used to develop a pro-forma statement, and if the statement has been developed carefully and thoughtfully, one may have great confidence in the statement itself, in its ability to provide information, and in its use as an integral part of the blueprint. The statement may be used and should be used as a criterion by which program implementation may be judged. However, if any key assumption is erroneous, the entire pro-forma statement becomes less useful—and in some cases harmful—in direct proportion to the magnitude of the error.

It may be taken as a general rule that if one is to err, if one is only slightly unsure of any facet of a program's income and expense or cash inflow and cash outflow factors, it is far better to err on the side of conservatism—to overstate expense and cash outflow factors and understate income and cash inflow factors—than to do the reverse.

INCOME STATEMENT VS. CASH FLOW

While the pro-forma income statement is more common than the pro-forma cash flow, the latter is generally more useful in blueprinting a program than the former. Both the pro-forma cash flow and the pro-forma income statement are analagous to a motion picture. They commence at a certain time and end at another certain time, and describe an estimate or projection of events which will occur during the period between the projection's commencement and its ending. Thus, a pro-forma income statement or pro-forma cash flow would be performed, again as examples, for a program's first, second, and third weeks of operation, or its first and third years of operation. The key factor is that it pertains to *a time period.* This is opposed to, as an example, a pro-forma balance sheet, which is analagous to a photograph, describing a projected financial situation at one specific point in time. For example, the same program's projected financial condition might be described by a pro-forma balance sheet for the end of the first year of operation. This projection would exist at that one moment of time, precisely one year from the commencement of the program. That is, it pertains to *a specific instant,* and not a time period.

The pro-forma cash flow and the pro-forma income statement are similar, in that they predict events that take place within periods of time rather than situations that will exist at points in time. It is with respect to their differences, however, that the usefulness of both projections is brought to light and the necessity for them is clarified.

The pro-forma income statement gives estimates of income and expenses; the pro-forma cash flow gives estimates of the cash that will flow into and out of the enterprise. Income is analagous but not identical to cash inflow; expense is analagous but not identical to cash outflow. A mathematical relation exists between the two, and its expression is the balance sheet—in the case of the present discussion, the pro-forma balance sheet. However, because detailed discussion of this relationship can be found in so many college- and graduate-level texts on accounting, the subject will not be pursued further in these pages. The essential point, simply, is that cash inflow is *not* identical to income, and cash outflow is *not* identical to expense.

As an example, Company A acquires an automated lathe with a useful life expectancy of ten years for use in its manufacturing plant. The cost of the machine is $100,000, and Company A, being in an excellent cash position at the time of the purchase, elects to pay cash for it. The expense associated with the acquisition of the machine is its depreciation, or $100,000 ÷ 10 = $10,000 a year for each of the next ten years, assuming straight-line depreciation. Cash outflow, on the other hand, is $100,000 in the first year and nothing in each of the next nine years. Considering the ten years as a whole, expense and cash outflow are identical. However, considering just the first year, cash outflow exceeds expense by a factor of 10: $100,000 as opposed to $10,000. A pro-forma cash flow states the $100,000 as a cash outflow in the first year; a pro-forma income statement states the $10,000 as an expense, namely "depreciation," in the first year. The ramifications of this fact are not only obvious, but critical.

To continue with the same example, Company A might have decided to finance the same automated lathe. Assuming that it were able to arrange five-year financing at an "add-on" interest rate of 8 percent calling for no down payment and equal monthly installments, its pro-forma cash outflow associated with acquisition of the machine is $28,000 for each year of the five-year period of financing. This amount includes payment both to interest and to reduction of principal. The pro-forma income statement, on the other hand, would show two expense items: depreciation, and interest applicable to the period in question.

If it is assumed that interest expense is divided equally over the five-year term of the financing agreement, Company A's pro-forma income statement shows a depreciation expense of $10,000 for each year of the machine's ten-year life and an interest expense of $8,000 for each of the five years of the financing contract. Again, expense equals cash outflow when the totality of the machine's ten-year life is considered, but in the first year, expense is $18,000 while cash outflow is $28,000, and in the sixth year, expense is $10,000 while cash outflow is zero.

The identical principle applies to the relationship between cash inflow and income. One of the basic principles of accounting practice is that income is recorded in the time period in which it is *earned*, but that does not necessarily coincide with the time period in which it is *received*. In fact, under practical circumstances, these time periods seldom coincide, unless the business is a strictly cash and carry operation, such as a fast-food restaurant or a newspaper stand.

Continuing with the same example, Company A has now put its new automated lathe to good use and has produced $100,000 worth of products. An offer for these items has been received from a buyer of the highest credit standing. Requested terms are "net 90," and Company A decides to accept the offer.

Company A's pro-forma income statement will show a sale, or income, in the first month of $100,000. However, its pro-forma cash flow will show a cash inflow of zero for that time period. Considering just the transaction described, the third month will show a cash inflow of $100,000, but an income of zero.

THE PRO-FORMA CASH FLOW

As a general rule, the pro-forma cash flow is somewhat more difficult to construct, more detailed, and more informative than the pro-forma income statement. Consequently, its development will be described first, although in actual practice the development of a pro-forma income statement will usually precede that of a pro-forma cash flow.

One of the benefits of the pro-forma cash flow statement, especially with regard to new programs, is that it provides a clear indication of the venture's working capital requirements. As a general rule, however, the time spans considered must be significantly shorter than those considered acceptable for a pro-forma income statement if this benefit is to be realized fully. For a restaurant operation, as an example, quarterly or yearly pro-forma income statements are typically adequate, whereas pro-forma cash flows should consist of a series of *weekly* projections. Yearly pro-forma income statements may be perfectly adequate for a manufacturing operation or service business, but pro-forma cash flows indicating less than monthly detail are seldom acceptable. In fact, some businesses, especially those engaged in arbitrage, actually perform pro-forma cash flows on an *hourly* basis. Of course, these businesses represent totally unique circumstances which are not applicable to the vast majority of enterprises, but their methodology does serve to emphasize the essential point: An acceptable pro-forma cash flow statement estimates cash inflows and outflows for significantly *shorter* periods of time than would be acceptable for the statement of estimated income and expense contained in a pro-forma income statement.

Exhibit 4.1 (on pages 40 and 41), together with its associated notes illustrates the preparation and use of the pro-forma cash flow. The critical importance of the pro-forma cash flow to the blueprint and the ultimate success of the blueprint's program warrant its careful study and understanding.

THE PRO-FORMA INCOME STATEMENT

The pro-forma income statement is a more common projection than the pro-forma cash flow, and its purpose is to predict the profitability of the project under contemplation. As has been mentioned, it is generally developed as a first step, and its indication of potential profitability is a major determinant of management's decision with respect to undertaking the project.

Exhibit 4.2 (on page 44) utilizes basic assumptions that are identical to those on which Exhibit 4.1 (Pro-Forma Cash Flow) is based, except where noted, and is an example of a developed pro-forma income statement.

THE EXPANDED PRO-FORMA INCOME STATEMENT

Of course, it is a rare venture that immediately experiences sales at the level predicted for it. Typically, a new business requires some period of time (the length of which will vary considerably from industry to industry, and even from operation to operation within an industry) for sales to grow to the level predicted. This sales curve is depicted in Exhibit 4.1 (Pro-Forma Cash Flow) in that it predicts $14,000 of gross sales for the first week of operations, with a decrease to $11,000 for the second week and a gradual building of sales till they attain the $14,000 level again in the seventh week—a situation which is not unusual and which results largely from the effects of grand opening promotions.

In light of this phenomenon, it would be singularly unfair to judge management performance at the operating level and during a business' initial phases by comparing actual income statement results with projected income statement results. Consequently, it is generally wise to construct a series of pro-forma income statements that reflect predicted sales growth so that they may be utilized to judge operating management efficiency not only when the business has attained predicted sales volume, but during its growth phase as well. In the case of the X Restaurant Corporation example, this has in a sense been accomplished in developing the pro-forma cash flow on a weekly basis, but it has been found that a comparison of predicted cash flow with actual cash flow can often be misleading about management efficiency, and that

PROGRAM ARITHMETIC: EXAMINING THE BOTTOM LINE

Exhibit 4.1: X Restaurant Corporation

	Week	0	1	2	3	4	5
Food Sales			7-	55	6-	6-	65
Beverage Sales			7-	55	6-	6-	65
Total Sales	(01)		14-	11-	12-	12-	13-
Cash Sales	(02)		56	44	48	48	52
Credit Sales	(03)						84
Total Cash Inflow			56	44	48	48	136
Food Inventory Replenishment	(04)	5	3-	25	19	21	21
Beverage Inventory Replenishment	(05)	3-		14	11	12	12
Cost of Credit	(06)						5
Payroll, Including Taxes	(07)	2-	45	35	38	38	42
Management Bonuses	(08)			2	1	1	2
Advertising and Promotion	(09)	3-		3	2	2	2
Linen and Laundry	(10)		2	2	2	2	2
Miscellaneous Supplies	(11)		1	1	1	1	1
Miscellaneous Variable Expense	(12)		2	1	1	1	2
Total Variable Outflows		85	8-	83	75	78	89
Contribution Inflow		(85)	(24)	(39)	(27)	(3-)	47
Rent, Including Utilities & Tel.	(13)	35				35	
Management Salaries	(14)	3	3	3	3	3	3
Entertainment	(15)		2	2	2	2	2
Insurance	(16)	13					
Legal and Accounting	(17)	5	1	1	1	1	1
Administration	(18)	1	1	1	1	1	1
Miscellaneous Fixed Expense	(19)	1	1	1	1	1	
Equipment Payments	(20)	12				12	
Total Fixed Outflows		7-	8	8	8	55	8
Net Cash Inflow	(21)	(155)	(32)	(47)	(35)	(85)	39
Cum. Net Cash Inflow	(22)	(155)	(187)	(234)	(269)	(354)	(315)

↑Peak Cash Outflow

THE PRO-FORMA INCOME STATEMENT
Pro-Forma Cash Flow (000's of $)

6	7	8	9	10	11	12	13	T:0-13
65	7-	7	7-	7-	7-	7-	7-	865
65	7-	7-	7-	7-	7-	7-	7-	865
13-	14-	14-	14-	14-	14-	14-	14-	173-
52	56	56	56	56	56	56	56	692
66	72	72	78	78	84	84	84	702
118	128	128	134	134	14-	14-	14-	1394
23	23	25	25	25	25	25	25	317
13	13	14	14	14	14	14	14	189
4	4	4	5	5	5	5	5	42
42	45	45	45	45	45	45	45	575
2	2	2	2	2	2	2	2	22
3	3	3	3	3	3	3	3	63
2	2	2	2	2	2	2	2	26
1	1	1	1	1	1	1	1	13
2	2	2	2	2	2	2	2	23
92	95	98	99	99	99	99	99	127-
26	33	3-	35	35	41	41	41	124
		35					35	14-
3	3	3	3	3	3	3	3	42
2	2	2	2	2	2	2	2	26
							13	26
1	1	1	1	1	1	1	1	18
1	1	1	1	1	1	1	1	14
1	1	1	1	1	1	1	1	14
		12					12	48
8	8	55	8	8	8	8	68	328
18	25	(25)	27	27	33	33	(27)	(-204)
(297)	(272)	(297)	(27-)	(243)	(21-)	(177)	(204)	

Notes to Exhibit 4.1: pro-forma cash flow
X Restaurant Corporation

(01) Assuming that total sales will consist of 50% food sales and 50% beverage sales, and further assuming that the restaurant will be opened unofficially two or three days prior to its official grand opening, primarily for the purposes of personnel training. For the sake of conservatism, no sales are projected for this period of time.

(02) Assuming that 40% of sales will be cash sales.

(03) Assuming that 60% of sales will be credit-card sales and that the cash representing those sales will be received in the fifth week from the week of the sale. Charges will be submitted to the credit-card company on a weekly basis.

(04) Assuming that food cost will be 35% of food sales, and that food inventory will be replenished weekly, with payment for food inventory replenishment being made seven days following delivery. It is further assumed that the restaurant will maintain a constant food inventory of approximately $3,000, and that food cost for its unofficially open period will approximate $500.

(05) Assuming that beverage cost will be 20% of beverage sales, and that beverage inventory will be replenished weekly, with payment for beverage inventory replenishment being made seven days following delivery. It is further assumed that the restaurant will maintain a constant beverage inventory of approximately $3,000, and that no beverages will be dispensed during its unofficially open period.

(06) Assuming that credit card company charges will be 6% of charges submitted.

(07) Assuming that payroll, including taxes, will be 32% of gross sales.

(08) Assuming that the restaurant's management will receive a bonus of 5% of weekly gross sales in excess of $10,000, and that this bonus will be paid on the basis of the previous week's performance.

(09) Assuming advertising and promotion expenditures at the rate of 2% of gross sales on a continuing basis, and further assuming the

THE PRO-FORMA INCOME STATEMENT

advanced expenditure of $3,000 for the grand opening promotion.

(10) Assuming expenditures for linen and laundry at the rate of 1.5% of gross sales on a continuing basis.

(11) Assuming expenditure for miscellaneous supplies at the rate of .75% of gross sales on a continuing basis.

(12) Assuming miscellaneous variable expenses at the rate of 1.25% to 1.30% of gross sales on a continuing basis.

(13) Assuming rent, including utilities and telephone, at the rate of $3,500 per month, payable monthly in advance. Although utilities and telephone will be payable at the month's end, these expenditures have been included in rental for the sake of conservatism.

(14) Assuming that a base salary of $300 per week will be paid to the restaurant's manager, including payroll taxes and benefits. This base salary is in addition to the performance bonus described in (08) above.

(15) Assuming that customer entertainment will be provided on one or two nights per week at a total cost of $200 per week.

(16) Assuming insurance at the rate of $100 per week, payable quarterly in advance.

(17) Assuming that legal and accounting fees will be budgeted and paid at the rate of $100 per week, with initial fees of $500.

(18) Assuming administrative, back-office expense at the rate of $100 per week on a continuing basis.

(19) Assuming that miscellaneous fixed expenses will occur at the rate of $100 per week on a continuing basis.

(20) Assuming that the total cost of equipment, furniture, and fixtures will be $60,000, and that the entire package will be leased to the restaurant at 8% add-on interest over a seven-year period.

(21) Indicating that the restaurant will be self-sustaining on a cash basis in its fifth week of operation.

(22) Indicating a peak cash outflow of $35,400 and working capital requirements in that amount.

Exhibit 4.2
X Restaurant Corporation Pro-Forma Income Statement (yearly)

	(000's of $)	(%)*
Food Sales	364.0	50.0
Beverage Sales	364.0	50.0
Total Sales	728.0	100.0
Food Cost	127.4	17.5
Beverage Cost	72.8	10.0
Cost of Credit	26.2	3.6
Payroll, including Taxes	233.0	32.0
Management Bonuses	10.4	1.4
Advertising and Promotion	14.6	2.0
Linen and Laundry	10.9	1.5
Miscellaneous Supplies	5.5	.8
Miscellaneous Variable Expense	9.1	1.3
Total Variable Expense	509.9	70.0
Contribution to Overhead and Profit	218.1	30.0
Rent, Utilities, and Telephone	42.0	5.8
Management Salaries	15.6	2.1
Entertainment	10.4	1.4
Insurance	5.2	.7
Legal and Accounting	5.2	.7
Administration	5.2	.7
Miscellaneous Fixed Expenses	5.2	.7
Interest (01)	4.8	.7
Depreciation (02)	6.0	.8
Total Fixed Expense	99.6	13.7
Net Profit Before Income Taxes	118.5	16.3

*The whole may not equal the sum of the parts because of rounding techniques employed.

Notes to Exhibit 4.2 (yearly) X Restaurant Corporation Pro-Forma Income Statement

(01) Assuming allocation of total interest with respect to equipment package financing on an equal, annual basis for the entire seven-year term of the financing agreement.

(02) Assuming depreciation of the entire $60,000 equipment package cost over ten years using the straight-line method of depreciation.

comparison of actual income statement results with predicted income statement results is a better indicator.

Exhibit 4.3 is representative of a series of pro-forma income statements that have been developed for this purpose by combining X Restaurant Corporation's pro-forma cash flow and pro-forma income statement.

THE BREAK-EVEN ANALYSIS

A blueprint's projections of profitability and cash flow are necessary to determine the wisdom of commencing a project and to judge performance during project development and implementation. Its projected break-even analysis, however, is useful primarily in that it presents a numeric and graphic description of the proposed project's operating risk.

It might be said that the pro-forma income statement is an answer to the question: "What income, expense, and net profit do I expect?" It might be said, too, that the pro-forma cash flow is an answer to the question: "What cash will the operation take in, what will it expend, and what net cash result can I expect?" If this is true, as it is in a large sense, then the projected break-even analysis might be said to be answers to the following questions:

- What happens to my profit if sales are lower or higher than I've anticipated?
- What sales do I have to make before I start to operate in the red?

The answers to these questions permit management to judge operating risk: The closer the projected break-even is to projected sales, the greater the operating risk; and the greater the operating risk, the less attractive the project.

Continuing with the example of X Restaurant Corporation, Exhibit 4.4 depicts graphically the project's break-even point: $332,000 per year, $27,667 per month, and $6,385 per week. Sales above those levels will give

Exhibit 4.3
X Restaurant
Corporation
Pro-Forma
Income
Statements (000's of $)

	1st Quarter	2nd Quarter and Thereafter*	1st Year	2nd Year and Thereafter
Food Sales	865	91-	3595	364-
Beverage Sales	865	91-	3595	364-
Total Sales	173-	182-	719-	728-
Food Cost	303	319	1258	1274
Beverage Cost	173	182	719	728
Cost of Credit	62	66	259	262
Payroll, Including Taxes	554	583	2301	233-
Management Bonuses	22	26	10-	104
Advertising and Promotion	35	37	144	146
Linen and Laundry	26	27	108	109
Miscellaneous Supplies	13	14	54	55
Miscellaneous Variable Expense	23	23	9-	91
Total Variable Expense	1211	1275	5033	5099
Contribution to Overhead and Profit	519	545	2157	2181
Rent, Utilities, and Telephone	105	105	42-	42-
Management Salaries	39	39	156	156
Entertainment	26	26	104	104
Insurance	13	13	52	52
Legal and Accounting	13	13	52	52
Administration	13	13	52	52
Miscellaneous Fixed Expense	13	13	52	52
Interest	12	13	48	48
Depreciation	15	15	6-	6-
Total Fixed Expense	249	249	996	996
Net Profit Before Income Tax	27-	296	1161	1185

*The whole may not equal the sum of the parts because of rounding techniques employed.

Exhibit 4.4
X Restaurant
Corporation
Break-Even Analysis (000's of $)

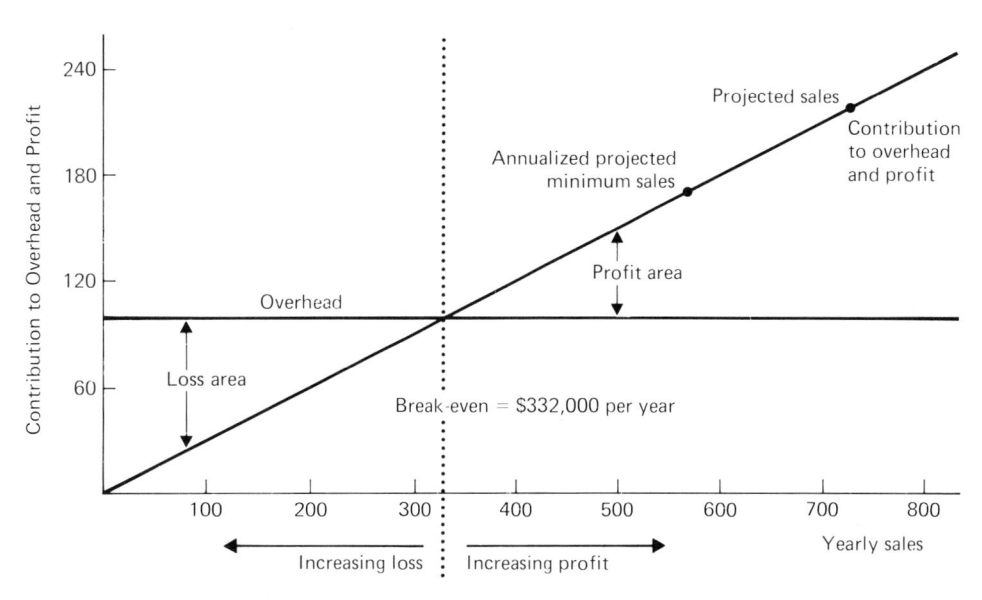

[Graph showing break-even analysis with Contribution to Overhead and Profit on y-axis (0-240) and Yearly sales on x-axis (0-800). Break-even = $332,000 per year. Labels include: Projected sales, Contribution to overhead and profit, Annualized projected minimum sales, Profit area, Overhead, Loss area, Increasing loss, Increasing profit.]

the project a net profit, and sales below those levels will mean a net loss for the project.

Examining this Exhibit allows management not only to determine the sales volume that the restaurant requires to break-even, but clearly to visualize the dynamic relationship of sales to profit and loss.

CAPITAL REQUIREMENTS

Of course, one item of information that is of critical importance to management's decision whether to embark on a project is the amount of capital that must be committed to it. Without this knowledge, in fact, it is impossible for management to ascertain ROI, and even the most thorough knowledge of predicted cash, income, and break-even performance is useless without prediction of total capital requirements. The management of X Restaurant Corporation, as an extreme example, may be thoroughly convinced that its restaurant project exhibits every probability of generating pre-tax profits at the $100,000 to $120,000 level. However, if investment required to generate those profits were $5,000,000 to $6,000,000, it is quite doubtful that management would decide to embark on the project. On the other hand, if total

Exhibit 4.5
Estimated Capital Required for Industry Entry by Branch Operator (200 seat capacity)

	Capital Required	
	Total Investment	**Cash Required**
Branchise Fee	$ 15,000	$ 15,000
Equipment Package*	75,000	25,000
Supplies (basic inventory)	10,000	10,000
Security on Leasehold	5,000	5,000
Working Capital	10,000	10,000
Total	$115,000	$ 65,000

*Balance of $55,000 on equipment to be financed over a five-year period.

required investment were $5,000 to $6,000, management's decision probably would be positive.

Exhibit 4.5 is an example of a format that might be used to present management with an estimate of capital that will be required to embark on the project of developing its new restaurant. It will be noted that cash requirements are stated at the $50,000 to $55,000 level, and total capital requirements are stated at the $110,000 to $115,000 level. When these data are combined with expected profitability levels, it might be predicted with some certainty that, all other things being equal, management's decision to embark on the project will be positive.

ADDITIONAL EXAMPLES

The remaining pages of this chapter contain additional examples of arithmetic projections that might have been prepared by a company with an interest in developing a "branchise" program. In this case, the parent company or "branchisor" is interested primarily in ascertaining income, expense, and investment levels for the typical "branchisee," and in developing a preliminary estimate of the "branchise" fee it might reasonably charge.

It should be restressed that during the preliminary, conceptual stages of any program—during the time prior to establishment of an operating record—the projections are necessarily assumptive. They are designed to provide the preliminary guidelines or estimates that will become a major factor in management's decision whether embarkation on the program is feasible.

ADDITIONAL EXAMPLES

For a hypothetical branch operator: performance and capital requirements and determination of preliminary branchise fee

Exhibit 4.6 Projected Operator's Profit and Loss at the $500,000 Gross Sales Level

	Dollars	Percent of Total Sales
Gross Sales	$500,000	100.0
Cost of Goods Sold:		
Food	219,000	43.8
Paper	10,000	2.0
	229,000	45.8
Gross Margin	271,000	54.2
Total Expenses	225,000	45.0
Net Profit before Taxes	$ 46,000	9.2
Expenses:		
Payroll and Taxes	$100,000	20.0
Laundry and Supplies	7,000	1.4
Utilities and Telephone	15,000	3.0
Property Taxes	3,000	.6
Insurance	2,000	.4
Maintenance and Repair	4,000	.8
Advertising	15,000	3.0
Office Expenses	1,000	.2
Royalties	20,000	4.0
Rent	40,000	8.0
Breakage	3,000	.6
Miscellaneous	2,000	.4
Professional Fees	1,000	.2
Interest Expense*	4,000	.9
Equipment Depreciation†	7,000	1.5
Total Expenses	$225,000	45.0

*Interest on the $50,000 equipment package financing reflects 8.5% to 9.0% add-on.
†Equipment depreciation is calculated on a straight-line depreciation basis over a ten-year period.

Exhibit 4.7 Projected Operator's Profit and Loss at the $600,000 Gross Sales Level

	Dollars	Percent of Total Sales
Gross Sales	$600,000	100.0
Cost of Goods Sold:		
Food	262,800	43.8
Paper	12,000	2.0
	$274,800	45.8
Gross Margin	$325,200	54.2
Total Expenses	259,200	43.2
Net Profit before Taxes	$ 66,000	11.0
Expenses:		
Payroll and Taxes	$114,000	19.00
Laundry and Supplies	7,800	1.30
Utilities and Telephone	16,800	2.80
Property Taxes	3,600	3.60
Insurance	2,400	.40
Maintenance and Repair	4,200	.70
Advertising	18,000	3.00
Office Expenses	1,200	.20
Royalties	24,000	4.00
Rent	48,000	8.00
Breakage	3,600	.60
Miscellaneous	2,400	.40
Professional Fees	1,200	.20
Interest Expense*	4,500	.75
Equipment Depreciation†	7,500	1.25
Total Expenses	$259,200	43.20

*Interest on the $50,000 equipment package financing reflects 8.5% to 9.0% add-on.

†Equipment depreciation is calculated on a straight-line depreciation basis over a ten-year period.

Exhibit 4.8 Estimated Turnkey Building and Equipment Cost (200 seat capacity)

Cost Factors	Dollars
Land	$135,000
Building	185,000
Lot Work	30,000
Equipment	75,000
Total Cost	$425,000

Exhibit 4.9 Estimated Capital Required for Industry Entry by Owner/Operator (200 seat capacity)

	Capital Required	
	Total Investment	**Cash Required**
Equipment Package*	$ 75,000	$25,000
Supplies (basic inventory)	10,000	10,000
Security on Leasehold	5,000	5,000
Working Capital	10,000	10,000
Total	$100,000	$50,000

*Balance of $55,000 on equipment to be financed over a five-year period.

Exhibit 4.10 Projected Cost of Placing One Branch Operator Into the Business

Cost to Operator		
Establishment Cost		$15,000
Cost to Parent*		
Site Selection	$2,500	
Recruitment advertising	1,000	
Recruitment Sales	3,000	
Schooling and Training	5,000	
Legal	1,000	12,500
Balance Retained by Parent Company		$2,500

*These costs will drop by economies of scale.

CHAPTER FIVE
EVALUATING FINANCE OPTIONS

EVALUATING FINANCE OPTIONS

A key section of the blueprint is exploration of financing availabilities for the project. Even if the company is well financed, it is important to consider possible sources of additional funds in order to avoid handicapping the business with oppressive financial requirements which may be unforeseen at the outset. Financing generally falls into two broad categories: loans and sales of equity.

BANK LOANS

Your prime loan source—generally most accessible to you—is your nearby bank or savings and loan association. Being local, they may be acquainted with you and your business, and familiar with your character, integrity, and stability. The guide they use for granting a loan is symbolized by three C's—Character, Capital, and Capacity to pay.

Under normal circumstances, most banks, will be receptive to your request for a reasonable loan. A bank loan is most advantageous because the interest rate is generally lowest.

You may obtain various types of loans from your local bank, but probably all of them will be either short-term loans (payable within about 90 days) or long-term loans (extending for as long as ten years).

"Popular" types of bank loans are:

▶ *Straight commercial loans* (usually 30 to 60 days): Based on a submitted financial statement, this loan is generally used for seasonal financing or inventory expansion.

▶ *Installment loans:* These are usually long-term loans, repaid on a monthly basis. These loans can be tailored to the needs of the business: for example, heavier repayments during peak months and smaller repayments during off-season periods.

▶ *Term loans:* Such loans have maturities of one to ten years and may either be secured or unsecured. Loan repayments may be made on almost any agreed-on basis—monthly, quarterly, semiannually, annually. Early repayments are often relatively small with a large final payment. Although many term loans are backed by collateral security, the lender ordinarily requires that current assets exceed current liabilities by a ratio of at least two to one.

▶ *Bills or notes receivable:* Promissory notes are often given for purchase of goods. These notes are called "bills receivable" or "notes receivable." They can usually be discounted—that is, purchased by the bank. Your account is credited with the amount of the note less the discount to the due date. The bank will collect from the note-makers when the note is due.

► *Warehouse receipt loans:* Under this form of financing, goods are stored in warehouses and the warehouse receipt is given to the bank as security for a loan to pay off the supplier. The borrower buys back portions of the inventory just as fast as he or she is able to sell merchandise.

► *Equipment loans:* Loans are made to finance the purchase of machinery or equipment. The lender usually retains title until installment payments have been completed.

► *Collateral loans:* These loans are based on such collateral as chattel mortgages on personal property, real estate mortgages, life insurance (up to cash surrender value of the property), or stocks and bonds. If your banker says "no," then contact your local Small Business Administration Office. They are geared to expedite loans (that are justifiable) for small businesses. They request, as your first step, that you initiate your loan request via your local bank. If the bank turns you down, SBA will undertake, in many instances, to "share" your loan with the local bank, assuming responsibility for 50 percent or more. The majority of banks (even those refusing your initial loan request) usually cooperate with SBA-sponsored loans.

► *Small Business Investment Companies:* SBIC's use partly private, partly federal money to provide capital for small businesses through loans, direct stock purchases, or debentures convertible into stock. This gives you a loan-procurement opportunity formerly available only to larger companies. These SBIC's are generally assisted by the Small Business Administration (authorized to buy up to $1,000,000 in debentures of an individual SBIC). Approximately 480 SBIC's are now in operation. Financing costs are generally higher than those of banks but often lower than other outside private sources. To obtain names and addresses of SBIC's in your area, write to Small Business Administration, Investment Division, Washington 25, D.C., or to National Association of SBIC's, 537 Washington Building, Washington 5, D.C.

GOVERNMENT FINANCING

Various departments and branches of government also offer the financing of businesses under certain circumstances. Such sources include:

► Small Business Administration
► Treasury Department
► Federal Reserve System
► Veteran's Administration

EVALUATING FINANCE OPTIONS

The federal government-sponsored "MESBIC" financing concept is explained in the following pages.

The MESBIC financing concept, sponsored by the United States Department of Commerce, is discussed at some length in the following section.

MESBIC This is an acronym for Minority Enterprise Small Business Investment Company, which designates a federal social program to encourage small business ownership by specified racial minorities. According to the Office of Minority Business Enterprise of the U.S. Department Of Commerce, in order for a business to qualify for financing by a MESBIC it must be controlled (at least 51 percent) by a "disadvantaged" person, which the Department defines as follows:

(1) The normal racial minorities—American Blacks, American Eskimos and Aleuts, American Indians, and Asian-Americans.

(2) Spanish extraction American citizens, including persons of Puerto Rican, Mexican, Cuban, and Spanish extraction.

(3) U.S. citizens who have served honorably while on active duty, other than training duty, in the U.S. Armed Forces anywhere in the world for at least one day on or after August 5, 1964 and prior to September 1, 1976, regardless of rank or grade.

(4) Other U.S. citizens whose participation in the free enterprise system is hampered due to social or economic considerations beyond their personal control—considerations such as formal education, financial capacity, geographic or regional distresses, social handicaps such as physical or mental difficulties, all of which restrict the individual from the opportunity to fully participate in our economic system.

While the company borrowing from a MESBIC must be controlled by a disadvantaged person, the MESBIC itself (the company which makes the loans and investments to such minority businesses) may be owned by non-minority stockholders. That is, the MESBIC program *does not* make any direct loans or grants or investments to minority-owned businesses; it finances small business investment companies, which, as MESBIC's make loans and investments to minority-owned businesses. The social purpose of the MESBIC program is to make it attractive for private capital to financially assist minority business by doing so in partnership with the federal government. The MESBIC itself is a privately owned, privately managed venture capital corporation; it can be organized by any person or group of persons or even a corporation—including non-American citizens and/or foreign corporations.

MESBIC organizers must invest a minimum of $300,000 in the company but an initial investment of $500,000 is more usual. With the funds available, the organizers of the MESBIC apply for a federal license. Initially, the government matches the organizers' money 100 percent, which means that for a $500,000 investment a MESBIC will have $1,000,000 to invest. After two-thirds of that $1 million of capital is invested in minority-controlled enterprises, the government may grant matching sums to the MESBIC at a ratio of up to $4 for every $1 of its own that a MESBIC invests. Thus, for that $500,000 investment a MESBIC could have $2,500,000 of capital available.

And that's not all. A "MESBIC" privately financed by a $500,000 investment and matched with $500,000 of Federal money may receive four other matching sums by selling to the government debenture bonds carrying low interest—with no personal endorsements or guarantee, no reserves or sinking funds, and interest only to maturity. The Office of Minority Enterprises states that "Because of these leveraging opportunities, we believe that a MESBIC, when fully leveraged and invested, may provide up to 25 times its capital in funds for disadvantaged businesses."

The reasoning behind this statement is shown by the following figures:

	Amount
Private capital investment	$500,000
S.B.A. funds to MESBIC	2,000.000
Total	$2,500,000
Four times from other sources (including SBA guaranteed bank loans)	$10,000,000
Total MESBIC funds	$12,500,000

In addition to the low money costs, MESBIC's have certain special tax advantages as follows:

▶ Gains on the sale of stock in a MESBIC are always a long-term capital gains.

EVALUATING FINANCE OPTIONS

- Loss on the sale of stock in a MESBIC is always a short-term (or ordinary) loss, regardless of the term held.
- Dividends received by the MESBIC from portfolio companies are 100% tax excludable.
- MESBIC profits on the sale of equity interests in porfolio companies are long-term gains to the MESBIC.
- MESBIC may create loss reserves on outstanding balances.
- MESBIC may create unlimited contingency reserves from profits.
- MESBICs may register as investment companies and receive pass-through authority under the Investment Act of 1940.

That is how a MESBIC investment company is organized and financed. And here is what MESBIC can do for minority-owned investment prospects:

- Make a direct investment in either a preferred or common stock, in a 50 percent-minority-owned business.
- Make a direct loan to such a business in the form of either a convertible debenture or an ordinary loan. The loan may be as long as 20 years but three to seven years is more usual.
- MESBICs may guarantee 100 percent of a loan from any third party.
- MESBICs can provide management and technical assistance for a fee.

Further "MESBIC" information is available by writing to:

The Mesbic Staff
Capital Development
Office of Minority Business Enterprise
U.S. Department of Commerce
Washington, D.C. 20230

OTHER AVENUES You can also obtain loans from the following sources:

- *Private capital:* Insert an ad in your local newspaper under "Capital Wanted." Through this

OTHER AVENUES

medium you may attract private investors who regularly consult this column for investment opportunities.

▶ *Factors:* In each community there are factoring firms which make loans to all types of businesses. Their standards are lower than those of banks, hence they are more inclined to extend you your desired loan (even though you may have been turned down by banks or government sources). Factors are recommended only as a last resort, since their interest rates are often excessive.

▶ *Insurance companies:* Many insurance firms maintain loan departments as important adjuncts to their business. Their rates (although generally higher than bank rates) are usually lower than that of factors and other loan sources.

▶ *Commercial investment companies:* There are many investment companies, privately constituted, that grant loans. You will find them listed in your local telephone directories (the yellow pages). Their rates are generally on a par with those rates of factors.

▶ *Leasing firms:* Leasing has become more and more prominent in recent years. Almost any type of product or equipment can now be leased. Leasing can:
  ▶ finance many aspects of your business—e.g., furniture, fixtures, machinery, equipment—giving you a period of three to five years to pay back (via small monthly payments);
  ▶ finance your customers (particularly if the product cost is comparatively high). You (as the seller) are immediately paid the full amount due. The customer pays the leasing company monthly over a period of years.

▶ *Floor-plan financing:* These are usually short-term loans applicable to merchandise in a store ("on the floor"). For example: boats, autos, appliances, etc.

CHAPTER SIX
EVALUATING LOCATION REQUIREMENTS

SITE SELECTION

Many blueprints are involved with external expansion. Whether the expansion is by a company-owned operation or by associated entrepreneurial operations, suitable sites must be obtained. Proper sites are so vital to most enterprises that it is often said that there are three factors that can almost assure the success of a business:

- ▶ Good location
- ▶ Good location
- ▶ Good location

Location of the business is important for a variety of reasons. In a retail business it is a matter of pedestrian traffic; for a manufacturer of heavy equipment it may be a matter of freight costs; for a service company it might be necessary to locate with "the trade." An intensive study of the important reasons for locating a business in a particular area is not highly important but may be something of a "science." Certain basic criteria from the experience of many companies should be examined in addition to those which may apply to a particular enterprise.

These basic criteria, generally applicable to any business, should be the starting point of a thorough site study:

1. *Selection of the city:* Here, management should be concerned with:
   a) the size of the city's trading area;
   b) the population composition;
   c) the emerging trends of the population,
   d) the trading areas' purchasing power;
   e) the distribution of purchasing power;
   f) number, size and quality of competition.

2. *General location within the city:* The particular location should be examined for:
   a) its power to attract attention, in the case of a retail business;
   b) again, the nature and quality of nearby competition;
   c) availability of access to the location;
   d) the impact of zoning regulations;
   e) direction of area expansion;
   f) general appearance of the area.

3. *The specific site:* Finally, the specific site to be acquired should be evaluated in the light of:
   a) the traffic count at the site;
   b) the ability of the site to intercept traffic destined for other locations;

c) the complementary nature of adjacent businesses;
d) availability of adequate parking facilities;
e) its cost.

A traffic count may reveal some interesting factors. Such a count is vital for a retail shopping operation. For service businesses, a traffic survey is also important but is often oriented to quality of the traffic, rather than quantity. In a business district, land values and rents are based on raw traffic counts. For a service business the traffic count should be refined into various components; not only how many people pass the location but also what kind of people are they?

When conducting a pedestrian traffic count, it should first be decided *whom* to count. What types of people should be included in the count? Is it important to split the survey between male and female? By age groupings? When should the count be taken? Make sure that individuals are counted only once, not both entering and leaving. Spot-interview random pedestrians as to the origin of their trip and their destination.

Keep in mind that the season, month, week, day, and hour all have an effect on a traffic survey. Density increases during pre-holiday times. Traffic may be heavier on factory paydays and on days when Social Security checks are received. Time of day must not be allowed to skew results; e.g., traffic flows accelerate during the noon hour. Local custom should also be considered as it may cause variations in traffic patterns.

After a day representative of normal traffic flow has been chosen, it should be divided into 30- and 60-minute intervals. Traffic can be counted in representative half-hour periods in the morning, noon, afternoon, and evening.

With the traffic survey accomplished and satisfactory, certain sources of information on the area should be explored. These sources would include the Planning Commission, the Zoning Board, Redevelopment Agency, Chamber of Commerce, Department of Public Works, Housing Authority, School Board, Street and Highway Departments, and the Parks and Recreation Departments.

It may be assumed that a service such as an employment agency, would be housed in an office building having a specific floor space and standardized layout. But in a branch operation this may not be the case. In the traditional city business area an office building might be available, but where business districts have migrated from the inner city to suburban shopping centers a free-standing building might house an employment service.

According to the Organization Plan, if the latter were the case then provision should be made for the creation of a distinctive building. This building would be standard for the chain and should be readily identifiable.

EVALUATING LOCATION REQUIREMENTS

The free-standing building specifications would have been standardized by the national parent company, but certain things must be checked at the actual location to determine whether local conditions would require any modifications. The company should check with the local zoning board to make sure that the use of this building would conform to current local housing restrictions and to determine which permits would be necessary.

The matter of exterior signs is of particular importance. The operation will benefit materially from the proper signs and their placement. The number, type, and size of permissible signs must be ascertained. Such types would include roof, free-standing, swinging, and facade. It might be possible to obtain variances from existing regulations from the zoning board but it is better to construct according to local requirements.

Generally, signs should be seen by the pedestrian as the site is approached. Distinctive signs and building construction are an important method of national advertising. In a suburban, free-standing operation there must be provision for sufficient parking, private and free of charge. Should this be impossible, the availability of inexpensive off-street parking facilities assumes basic importance—the lack of private parking facilities can be offset, in large degree, by the proximity of commercial parking lots, public garages, or municipal parking facilities.

To draw traffic from a highway system, the approach to the site should not be from:

- limited access, fast-moving (40 mph-plus) highways;
- highways with center dividers;
- hills and ramps;
- left-turns in or out of the site against heavy traffic, unless controlled by traffic lights.

To enhance the free-standing location the site should provide:

- several wide curb cuts;
- easy access to the building from the parking area;
- convenient parking "slots" sufficient for the anticipated volume;
- employee parking.

There are marketing refinements to be considered. For example: What are the compounded growth rates of the territory, both for the labor market relative to population and for the producers relative to their gross national product contribution? Are the rates accelerating or, perhaps, negative? What is the history and present "temperature" of labor relations? What is the mobility of this labor force? How is the labor market divided by education, by racial balance? Is it skilled or unskilled, organized or unorganized? What is the general structure of the household income?

CHAPTER SEVEN

EVALUATING ADVERTISING AND PROMOTION

ADVERTISING AND PROMOTION

Virtually any type of project must be marketed. The more effective the marketing, the better the potential profit. Hence, advertising and promotion are critical components in blueprinting a program. They can help to:

- ► accelerate growth;
- ► set a high profit margin;
- ► establish a formula for continuity of the business, based upon a successful promotional formula. This enables projection of results through the use of similar promotional data at similar costs. Thus, a reliable "bottom line" figure can be extrapolated.

The corporate image, as projected by the promotional plan, is also important in selling the program or hindering its implementation.

Publicity and public relations are also functions of the Advertising/Promotion Department. The objective of these efforts is to project an attractive image of the business and to encourage community involvement with it.

PRE-OPENING AND GRAND-OPENING PROCEDURES

For effective operations, a grand-opening program is virtually indispensable. It helps give the enterprise a proper start and momentum, it promotes effective publicity and it's good public relations exposure. In many small communities the mayor will often officiate in "cutting the ribbon" and local newspapers will devote extensive space to publicizing the grand opening.

Most important is the effect of the grand-opening program has in helping to boost morale of the new operation's management. The grand opening is so important to the success of a business that its projected cost should be incorporated in the blueprint as an essential part of program funding.

The new venture will need certain selling tools to acquaint the local community of its existence and to induce people to try the products and services. Traffic alone cannot be depended upon. There are certain basic elements which comprise pre-opening and grand-opening promotions. These can be prepared by the parent organization and incorporated into the Distribution Operations Manual. The following list includes several of these:

1. As soon as the site is leased, signs should be displayed prominently upon the structure, announcing the impending opening. The copy and designs for the signs should be included in the grand-opening package.

2. A publicity release, to be placed in newspapers in the operator's territory, shortly after the contract is signed, announcing the appointment of Mr. or Ms. X as a distributor. The parent organization will submit a representative story which will contain the suggested information.

3. About two weeks prior to the opening, or as soon as a firm date has been established, signs should be placed in the window, fixing the date of the grand opening, and advertising door prizes, specials, give-aways, etc. Celebrities who are expected to attend the opening should be highlighted.

4. Teaser ads: A series of attention-provoking teaser ads (small space ads) to be placed in local newspapers, announcing the coming opening.

5. Five days prior to the grand opening, an ad should be placed in appropriate newspapers announcing the forthcoming opening. The newspaper ad for the grand opening, should be approximately 1/4 of a page in size and should feature basic specials. This ad might announce drawings for door prizes (if they are legal in the area).

6. Radio spot announcements: These are quite inexpensive in most smaller communities and should be considered, particularly during the grand opening.

7. Handbills: To be placed under windshield wipers of parked autos in the community, and also in industrial parking lots, announcing the grand opening.

8. Roving vehicle: This can be an antique auto, with eye-catching decorations. It will contain signs about the grand opening. The driver will wear a colonial-motif hat and shirt and will distribute introductory get-acquainted coupons. Also, when the auto is parked in front of the unit it doubles as a stationary billboard.

9. Itinerant clown: This type of promotion has been used with fine results. A clown moves around town . . . performing antics to attract passersby, children, etc., and handing out announcements about family specials offered during the grand opening.

10. The day before the grand opening, the site should be decorated with grand-opening banners and pennants, which may be rented locally. This decorative material should be left up for one week.

11. Attractive girls, recruited from the local high school, might be employed to give out free door prize tickets in and around the areas during the opening week.

In addition to those of the above activities that will be ongoing during opening week, others should be arranged for the grand opening itself. For example:

1. Preview party: This idea can be especially effective in small towns. The press and important local people are invited, during opening day, for a preview party, with free refreshments provided. In small communities, even the mayor may be induced to attend, resulting in substantial publicity.

2. Women's clubs: Invite these groups to the grand opening. Guests to include: Local Women's Club officers, church officials, Ladies Auxiliary leaders, etc. Personalized invitations should be sent to them, for they represent influence leaders in the community.

3. Treasure chests: A "treasure chest" is placed in the store and a key is given with each purchase. Those having "lucky" keys that open the chest win prizes. This entire project can be purchased inexpensively (for about $60, including 1,000 keys).

Timetable

The purpose of Exhibit 7.1 is to present an overall view of the grand-opening tasks, showing the major items in relation to time and to each other. The primary advantage of such a timetable is that it prevents the overlapping that would result in conflict; it puts the priorities where they belong. It is at best a guide. It has flexibility and can be adjusted and embellished to accommodate special circumstances.

Checklists

Notice that, at certain periods on the timetable, there are boxes labeled "Checklist A," "Checklist B," etc. These are a very important part of the timetable; they tell what to do at what time before the opening.

These checklists are presented as Exhibits 7.2 through 7.5. They contain all items included in the timetable plus items too numerous to be placed on the chart but no less important. Certain items are discussed in greater detail in the sections following the checklists.

PRE-OPENING AND GRAND-OPENING PROCEDURES

Exhibit 7.1 Pre-Opening Time Table

Months Before Opening				
5 Months	4 Months	3 Months	2 Months	1 Month

Weeks before grand opening of store: 21 20 19 18 17 16 15 14 13 12 11 10 9 8 7 6 5 4 3 2 1 0

- **Weeks 20–16:** Agreement / Financing / Site selection / Lease / Plans and specifications / Approval of plans / Select contractor
- **Weeks 14–13:** Franchise training at home office.
- **Weeks 11–2:** Early Publicity
- **Weeks 2–0:** Grand opening Publicity-advertising
- **Weeks 15–7:** Construction — Inspection — Inspection
- **Weeks 15–6:** Fixtures ordered — Fixtures installed
- **Weeks 12–5:** Obtain advisors and services
- **Weeks 8–4:** Merchandise ordered/delivered
- **Weeks 5–2:** Hire and train help
- **Weeks 2–0:** Start-up personnel from home office
- **Weeks 2–1:** In-store franchise training / Informal opening
- **Week 0:** Formal grand opening

Checklist A — Checklist B — Checklist C — Checklist D

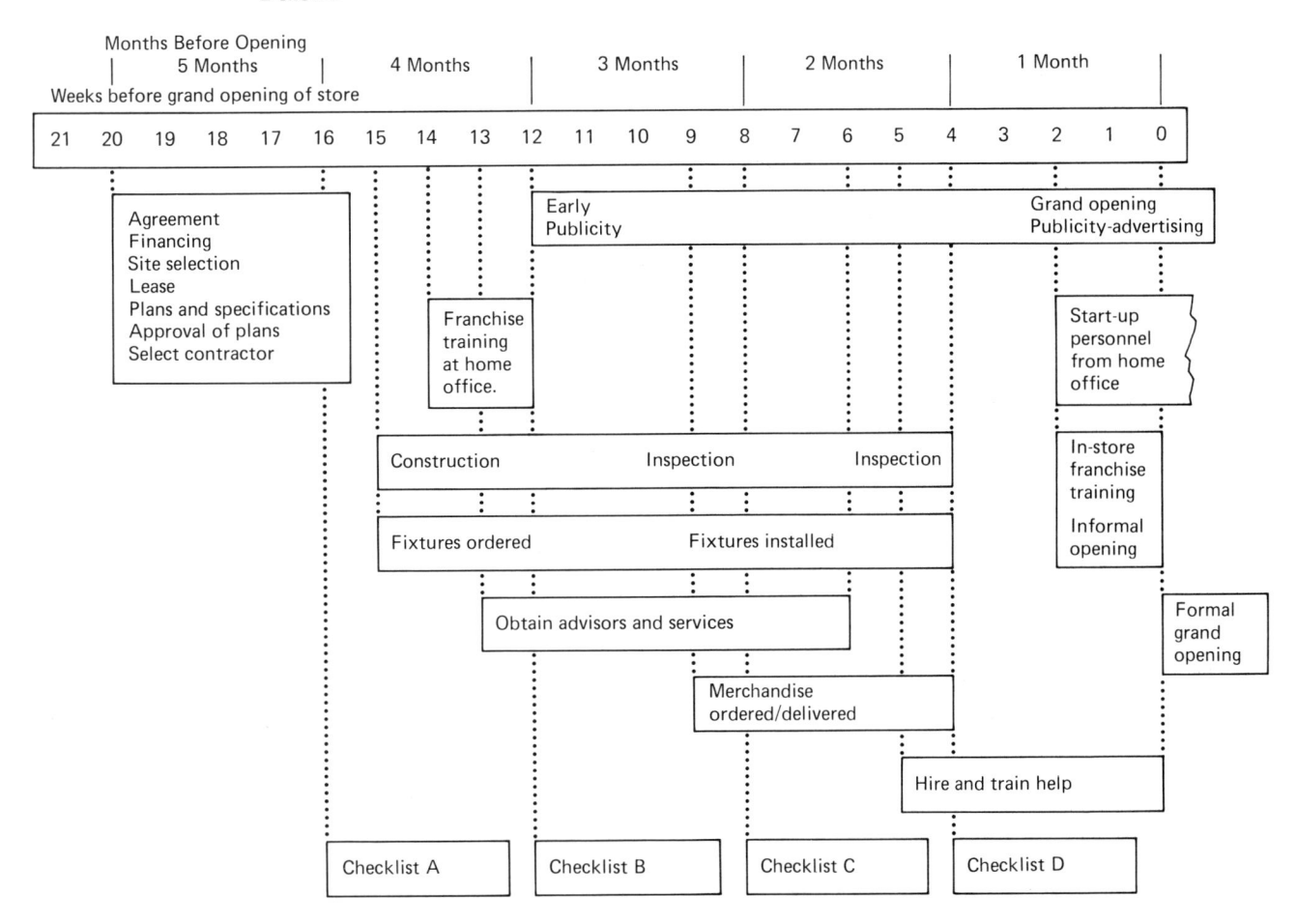

Exhibit 7.2 Checklist A (to be done three to four months prior to the grand opening)

_____ Approval of construction plans by various municipal departments.

_____ Construction begins.

_____ Two weeks franchisee training at home office.

EVALUATING ADVERTISING AND PROMOTION

_____ Fixtures and equipment ordered by home office.

_____ Contact post office for exact mail address.

_____ Obtain advisory services.

_____ Preliminary arrangements for essential services and utilities.

_____ Register name.

_____ Establish bank account.

_____ Apply for necessary licenses.

_____ Construction progress inspection.

_____ Select insurance program.

_____ Arrange for security service.

Exhibit 7.3 (to be done two to
Checklist B three months prior to
grand opening)

_____ Construction continues.

_____ Release early publicity announcing appointment as franchisee and construction of store. Find form for this story in the manual.

_____ Put COMING SOON sign in window. See Promotion section of the manual.

_____ Fixtures start arriving.

_____ Check on services and utilities.

_____ Inventory is ordered by home office. List furnished.

_____ Obtain legally required inspections (municipal).

_____ Check floor-covering installation date with contractor to be ready for installation of equipment.

_____ Obtain IRS forms and schedules and withholding permits.

PRE-OPENING AND GRAND-OPENING PROCEDURES

_____ Obtain employment wage-and-hour regulation sheets, workman's-compensation notices, etc., for posting.

_____ Join selected local organizations, including Chamber of Commerce and Better Business Bureau.

Exhibit 7.4 (to be done one to
Checklist C two months prior to
            grand opening)

_____ Inventory starts arriving.

_____ Check incoming merchandise against shipping lists. Notify home office and supplier of shortages and damage by registered mail.

_____ Begin to stock shelves in accordance with layout and plans by home office.

_____ Check on sales tax permits.

_____ Arrange balance of services, such as laundry, trash disposal, window cleaning, etc.

_____ Frame permits and licenses. Display same.

_____ Start to hire, bond, and train appropriate personnel. See chapter on Personnel.

_____ Establish list of sources of emergency repair—plumbing, air conditioning, etc.

Exhibit 7.5 (to be done during
Checklist D month prior to grand
             opening)

_____ Home office training director or field supervisor arrives to give "start-up" assistance and to stay through the grand opening.

_____ Two weeks in-store franchisee training.

EVALUATING ADVERTISING AND PROMOTION

_____   Informal opening (unadvertised). Start ten-day "dry run" before Grand Opening.

_____   Put NOW OPEN sign in window.

_____   Continue employee training as needed.

_____   Check on housekeeping, have windows washed.

_____   Study grand-opening program in Sales Promotion section of this manual.

_____   Put grand-opening program into effect.

_____   Formal grand-opening ceremonies.

EFFECTIVE LOW-BUDGET PROMOTIONAL CONCEPTS

The success of any business expansion program is:

- ▶ *not* the amount of "geography" of a country that you have allocated for a local operation.
- ▶ *not* the number of colored tacks that you may have attached to your office sales map.
- ▶ *not* the great numbers of units you have acquired and to which you proudly point.

No, *it is none of these.* Whether you have only two units or 250 units, the success of the program is based only on the success of the local operations.

Certain things can be done to assist in the success of these local units. For example:

▶ *It is possible* for each local operation to acquire 100 or more branch offices functioning to show and sell company products or services throughout the local area, day-in, day-out.

▶ *It is possible* for the local unit to acquire hundreds of salespeople—in most instances the influential people of the community—by obtaining participation of all clubs, associations, and church groups in the area.

▶ *It is possible* to add three, six (and even more) new, separate businesses to the local operation—each being highly profitable—so that, in effect, there is a multiple sales potential of at least that number.

EFFECTIVE LOW-BUDGET PROMOTIONAL CONCEPTS

▶ *It is possible* to give dealers the advantage of having greater inventory—and greater turnover—without needing to physically increase their inventory.

▶ *It is possible* to get the company's *best* customers to come to the place of business, in *large groups*—perhaps 100 of them at a time, or even more—and to remain there for an hour or more, listening to speakers concerning company products and services.

▶ The business can reach every prospect in the community—at their own home or business—thereby reaching the *total market*. And it can do so *without adding a single salaried employee*.

▶ Products and services can be displayed and discussed in as many as 100 homes a day in the area, on a continuing basis, with a sales potential averaging $500 per home.

▶ Finally, any product can be "revisualized" in a selling technique, so that instead of it being "just a product" it becomes instead, a "rare jewel," something that everyone wants to buy.

These statements sound astonishing but they are concepts now in use by many major, enterprising companies, worldwide, who have earned hundreds of millions of dollars by applying them. The following sections explain how you, too, may apply them.

BRANCH OFFICES

To repeat: as many as 100 branch offices can be acquired in the operating area. There are several methods to accomplish this.

▶ Use so-called "catalog corners." This means that tables to which the company catalog is attached are placed in other (noncompeting) stores throughout the area—with the participating storekeeper obtaining a commission on referrals coming from his or her store. Also such catalogues are placed in train and plane depots, where large crowds congregate. Thus, *market wide* exposure is achieved on a prestigious level—in effect, through dozens of "branch offices"—without increasing overhead.

Such well known stores as Sears-Roebuck Co., J. C. Penney, and even Macy's Department Store have featured such catalog corners, with extremely profitable results.

▶ Companies that have no catalogs—such as service-type operations—place an attractive stand-up sign in noncompetitive stores throughout the area, with each participating dealer receiving a commission on referrals. This plan has been used for a service-type operation that offered a gardening service to homes. The results greatly increased sales, besides providing valuable advertising and public relations exposure.

▶ Place *displays* of company products or services in noncompeting stores in the area. For example: a cosmetics manufacturer placed cosmetic displays in drugstores; a candy maker placed candy displays in drug stores; a wig-maker contacted all barber and beauty salons in the area and thus acquired literally hundreds of "branch" offices; a boutique wholesaler contacted all hotels in the marketing area, installing boutique displays in their lobbies. In a hotel, a local pipe shop installed displays of its expensive pipes. Also, an art gallery displayed samples of its paintings. The same idea is applicable to many types of products—and to services, too.

▶ A franchise business that used high-pressure spraying equipment to clean roofs, chimneys, gutters, and driveways participated with a national department store chain to promote these services to their customers.

▶ To obtain additional "branch offices" place advertisment listing in telephone books throughout the trading area, not only in the particular city where the business is located. This presents you to inaccessible areas that need, but do not know where to obtain, your company's products or services.

If it is thought that this "branch-office" concept is too novel, too unorthodox, consider this fact: In New York City, one of the most prestigious stores in the field of men's apparel is Brooks Brothers. The store is known world-wide. Their patronage is so highly selective that it's been humorously stated that one needs to show proof of a bank account of at least $100,000 plus impeccable character references before they'll even allow you to buy from them! Yet, recently, this self-same firm—with all its dignity—has been renting hotel rooms throughout the country in which to display and sell their merchandise (similar to the way suits from Hong Kong have been sold). Again, they have given themselves the benefit of many "branch offices."

How to get clubs, churches, and other associations in a community to actively promote the sales of company products or services? The reason such organizations will cooperate is because each has a program to earn monies to finance their charity and other worthwhile projects. That means that hundreds of their members will contact their friends, neighbors, and others to sell company products.

As an example: one firm, in the lighting bulb field, obtained such participation from the Junior Chambers of Commerce—also from the Kiwanis, Lions, Rotary, and Elks clubs (this resulted in over 1,000 sales people!). Sales totalled $400,000 just from these sources.

Even Girl Scouts and Boy Scouts will knock on doors throughout the area, projecting the impact of their wonderful, heartwarming personalities, just selling for your company.

MAIL-ORDER DEPARTMENT

This enables the company to reach customers who would not ordinarily come to the store. A new dimension is achieved for the business and complete market coverage is obtained. For example, a unit in the bookstore field added a mail-order department which did better than retail store sales—in fact, it helped to increase retail sales. Another company, in the jewelry field, also built up a thriving mail-order business offering gift and jewelry items. What can be mail-ordered for your current business?

RENT-IT DEPARTMENT

In addition to selling company products, consider *renting* them. Here is a simple idea that has helped many small businesses to multiply their sales. The success of this plan is based on a simple point of psychology . . . many people hesitate to commit themselves to a big-purchase item but they're willing to spend less money to try it out. Generally, they end up by buying it. For example:

Appliance stores rent TV sets for so much per day, with these payments credited to the purchase price.

Office machine stores rent typewriters, bookkeeping machines, dictaphone machines, etc. A music shop rents pianos.

This idea has been used by auto dealers, hardware stores, sporting goods stores—practically any type of business.

ADDED RELATED PRODUCTS OR SERVICES:

Evaluate the nature of company products or services. What related product or service can be added that will enable your operation to increase profits from selling to the same customer?

As an example: a tobacco store added boutiques and greeting cards. In the service field, a business that cleaned roofs, driveways, chimneys, and patios through spray-on of water and chemicals added other home-related businesses, such as spray-on fire deterrent chemicals, spray-on paints and even customized concrete steps.

Think about your company products or services. What related products or departments can be attached to your company to enhance its earning potential?

Still another approach for reaching out-of-area prospects, to penetrate the total market, is to add mobility to the business. Equip a motor van to sell and service the customers right at their own homes. For example, there was the "Pet Mobile" of a pet shop that was fully-equipped to groom dogs right in the van . . . and made regular rounds of customers' homes. There was also the "Handyman Mobile" of a hardware dealer that contacted homes in each area to perform their needed handyman services and was fully equipped for most jobs.

Another example is the spray-on painting of homes offered by a paint dealer. A motor van was specially equipped to perform this work. Many have heard of Snap-On Tools. The business of this highly successful organization is essentially built around trucks bringing needed tools and accessories to garages, gas stations, and auto dealers on a regular schedule.

PROVIDING THE ADVANTAGES OF GREATER INVENTORY—WITHOUT HAVING TO PHYSICALLY INCREASE INVENTORY

This concept, on its face, sounds preposterous! However, a company in the bookstore field accomplished just that. Normally as much as $60,000 in inventory is required to equip such a bookstore, and this would be altogether too costly for the planned small type of book operation.

The sponsor's distribution methods were improved—computerized—so that stock replacement shipments were made on the same day, instead of 30 days later. Thus the small dealer, with the same assortment of books, could now order one-fifth the usual requirements. This meant that now a store with as little as $10,000 in inventory could be operated. It meant, furthermore, that inventory turnovers, instead of occurring only twice a year, could occur as many as ten times per year.

A special department was arranged in each dealer's store, with the sponsor's catalog displayed and catalog orders invited. The catalog contained $250,000 in inventory, giving each dealer the benefit of showing that amount in merchandise to customers. Hence, this same small $10,000-inventory store became, in effect, a potential $250,000-inventory store, surpassing the stock of any of its competitors.

Such chain-store giants as Sears-Roebuck and Montgomery Ward are based on catalog-ordering departments.

HOW TO GET THE BEST CUSTOMERS TO COME TO THE BUSINESS LOCATION IN LARGE GROUPS

Convention exhibits, such as business conventions, associations, trade unions, and so on, attract groups of people who are potential customers. To illustrate the possibilities there is the example of a company which provides record-keeping systems for the medical profession. Rather than sell one system at a time on a physician-to-physician basis, they contacted groups of physicians at conventions, where they were able to talk and sell to as many as 100 or more prospects at one time. Supplementing this, they set up exhibits at professional conventions.

There is another example of a business in the motivational field which contacted labor unions—a type of group that most organizations ignore as customers. But today, unions have large funds available to help "uplift" members, and by contacting only three unions (which is only a small fraction of the total in this country) the company was able to sell motivational programs for use by some six thousand union members.

Another approach is to use methods that cause large groups of people to come to the outlets. For instance:

▶ Conduct Seminars: A company in the communications field manufactured and sold interoffice telephones that replaced the public telephone system. Their position was that this equipment enabled large firms, such as department stores and other large organizations, to save substantial monies and obtain better service. A seminar was announced to foremost companies among the *Fortune Magazine* "400", which comprise some of the larger organizations in the United States). A substantial number of top executives attended. The subject that attracted them was: "Achieving Better Communications in Your Organization and Saving as much as $50,000 a Year." In fact, the subject and the authoritative panel were so appealing that they would gladly have paid a fee to attend!

▶ Conducting exhibits is another means to bring company products or services before large groups. Such exhibits held in trade shows, conventions, state and city fairs and the like, are good prospects. Examples of such exhibits include:

▶ A flower shop advised people about various kinds of flowers and floral arrangements and how they could be used for home display, table decorations, etc., to fit any desired need.

▶ Furniture and decorating shops exhibited pictures of newest furniture designs, discussed varied period designs, the combining of colors, etc.

► A hardware store conducted a special showing of items that help save space around the home.

HOW TO REACH EVERY PROSPECT IN THE COMMUNITY—BOTH HOMES AND BUSINESSES—WITHOUT ADDING A SINGLE SALARIED EMPLOYEE

Direct-to-the-customer marketing is a multibillion dollar business in the United States. An example that comes to mind is a company that sold water softeners to homes. It charged $300 for this equipment. In the same community, there was a department store that sold similar equipment for half the price. Yet . . . the sales of the company were triple that of the local department store. Why? One approach was to passively wait for customers to come by and to ask to buy the product. The other approach was to *demonstrate* the benefits of the apparatus to prospects in their own homes.

Some of the largest department stores and other organizations in the United States now recognize the effectiveness of direct-to-customer approaches. These include such renowned stores as Macy's, Gimbels, and others. They now offer in-home service for such items as interior decoration, upholstery, draperies, modernization, furniture, apparel and dozens of other products and services.

HOW TO GET YOUR PRODUCTS DISCUSSED AND DISPLAYED IN AS MANY AS 100 HOMES, ON A CONTINUING BASIS, WITH A SALES POTENTIAL OF $500 PER HOME!

This is a direct-selling method that has proved highly effective and profitable in the United States—the so-called "party plans." Homemakers by the hundreds and even thousands are recruited to invite friends, relatives, and neighbors to their homes where company products or services are displayed and discussed.

Sales averaging as high as $500 per house "party" have been reported, as a result of this technique. One organization, Tupperware, uses party plans as the core of their entire business. They've built a mammoth international business selling Tupperware almost exclusively through party plans.

TAKE AN OBJECTIVE LOOK AT YOUR OPERATION

A walk in the famous "pushcart" section of Manhattan with its ramshackle carts showing a great variety of merchandise can reveal some unique selling techniques. On such a walk one stand in particular attracted my attention. The merchandise baffled description. It was really a pile of junk—yes, actually so. For example: an old razor, a rusty handle for a drawer, an old key, a broken toy, etc. Who would ever buy the stuff? But the pushcart proprietor didn't look at his merchandise as junk. He handled each piece as if it was a rare jewel, picking up the rusty razor, for example, with spotlessly white tissue paper, almost like a jeweler displaying a rare diamond. Somehow the value image communicated itself to people around the stand. They started buying the rusty nail, the razor, the old key, and the old picture frame. They didn't buy the product, they bought the dream—not what the product was, but what it could be!

Now look at your company's business. If it is a hardware store, is it just another store, competing with many similar ones? If so, does it depend on competitive prices—or perhaps neighborhood loyalty—for patronage? Neither of these alternatives is reliable.

Now, utilizing this same hardware store, plan to sell "systems" rather than "products." Change its concept to a "store for better living"—*Better living* that offers:

- Better equipped kitchens
- Increased home conveniences
- Durability, safety
- Home security
- Increased home value

By selling *systems,* one dramatizes the effect of company products—the things they can do rather than the things they are. It makes possible the sale of products in *clusters*—a number at a time instead of one-by-one. It also enables the store to offer a concept that no competitor has. Think about the company operation; what systems can be offered? Well, consider these examples:

- A business in the lighting field, selling lamps of all types, offered a complete lighting system for homes and offices. It sold "better vision" and "better working efficiency"—themes rather than products.

- A manufacturer of door locks offered a complete home security system" (installed) which provided proper locks and other security precautions for the *entire* home.

- A distributor of record-keeping books offered a complete "business management system," including all books and forms required to assist businesspeople in both the keeping of proper records and the management of their businesses.

All these new concepts give an "added dimension" to a business. Substantial business is obtained through the promotions used outside the store, bringing the products or services direct to the prospective purchaser in the most dramatic, effective manner.

Finally, and very important, consider the parent establishment: Is the sponsoring company properly set up? Have the proper personnel been hired to provide local distributors with the backup they need? Is the company equipped to service them efficiently in production and distribution? Can orders be filled promptly? Inability to provide what the customer expects can quickly shatter the entire expansion program.

One company in the infra-red industrial heating field is a prime example. The first group of distributors, after they had received their training, went out into their respective territories and achieved over a million dollars in orders almost immediately. The sponsor had not expected this volume and was not geared to manufacture at that rate. Consequently, the orders were either delayed or didn't get filled. The morale of the distributing organization crumbled and the entire program—which should have been extremely successful—failed.

Another example of the imperative need of the sponsor's home office to maximize its efficiency is that of the bookstore client to whom we previously referred. In commencing their program, the sponsors were appalled to realize that it would require at least $100,000 in inventory to properly equip each store . . . a sum that was much too high for the small distributors they were seeking. Analyzing the situation, they realized that such a large inventory was needed because their distribution methods were completely out of date; that it would take weeks and often months before the local operation could receive replacement stock. This would cause the local unit to overload itself with merchandise to make sure that it didn't run short.

The sponsor solved this problem by computerizing the distribution procedures; reorders could now be dispatched the same day as received. The result was that the local distributor could now get by with as little as $25,000 in inventory and yet be able to offer the same assortment of merchandise as the competition. By "cleaning their own house," then, the parent company was able to convert a nonfeasible expansion program into an efficient operation.

TAKE AN OBJECTIVE LOOK AT YOUR OPERATION

To further reduce the need for extensive inventory, the same parent company also established a catalog corner in the store of each local unit. These catalogs comprised some 200 pages and 15,000 products, a total merchandise inventory exceeding $300,000 in merchandise value. Thus, with only $25,000 of inventory it was possible to show and sell from a total stock valued at $400,000. No competition was able to equal this. The distributor was able to increase sales with the same overhead.

CHAPTER EIGHT

REQUIRED ORGANIZATION PERSONNEL

ORGANIZATION Let's say Company X has conceived a unique merchandising method. While there is every indication that it will be profitable on a local level, its nature is such that a national or international network is required to maximize the benefits it offers. With this in mind, a blueprint is undertaken for the development of the concept as a local branch program.

Company X has identified five stages through which the program will progress:

1. Planning a prototype operation, commencing immediately and continuing until approximately a month to a week prior to the Grand Opening of the prototype;

2. Operating the prototype for a six-month period to ascertain the validity of the concept and to develop operating data in financial and other areas which can be projected for future units;

3. Developing the operator program based on the prototype's performance;

4. Preparing for the sale of local territories and administration of the resulting operator network;

5. Selling local business units and operating and administering the system.

Recognizing that organizational requirements will differ in each of these stages, Company X has developed five separate tables of organization, one for each stage. Stage 1 includes only one executive and a board of directors, with the intent to rely on the directors for advisory areas.

As the program is implemented, and organizational requirements grow, personnel are added at each stage, each with a clearly defined function and reporting responsibility. When Stage 5 is reached the Company is able to perform efficiently with its own personnel.

Company X has also defined the needed corporate functions at each stage of its growth and has divided them into project stages—such as developing a blueprint for the program.

The project stages are defined as follows:

1. Develop blueprint

2. Select board of directors

3. Arrange financing

ORGANIZATION

4. Establish corporation
5. Determine advisors
6. Select prototype site
7. Design prototype and establish design criteria
8. Select contractor for prototype
9. Construct prototype
10. Conduct prototype grand opening
11. Develop operating manual
12. Develop training manual
13. Develop sales promotion package
14. Develop program sales package
15. Develop sales materials and operations package
16. Develop accounting and control system
17. Develop operator's agreement
18. Develop business newsletter
19. Hire personnel as follows:
    a) Prototype manager
    b) Prototype personnel
    c) Training director
    d) Bookkeeper
    e) Program director
    f) Program Sales manager
    g) Purchasing director
    h) Field service representatives
    i) Advertising and promotion manager
    j) Program salesmen
    k) General counsel
    l) Staff and research assistant
    m) Real-estate manager
    n) Marketing director
    o) Controller
    p) Public relations manager

REQUIRED ORGANIZATION PERSONNEL

The continuing functions are defined as follows:

1. Advertising
2. Accounting/Control
3. Finance
4. Local operator sales
5. Operator field support
6. Local operator relations
7. Site selection
8. Operator training
9. Legal
10. Marketing
11. Personnel
12. Prototype operations
13. Public relations
14. Purchasing
15. Research
16. Sales promotion

To be certain that the planned organization is capable of completing each of the defined projects and performing each of the continuing functions optimally, each project and each function has been charted with respect to the stage in which it is scheduled to occur. The plan is also charted with respect to a chain of command, which is directly responsible for the project or function (Line Chain), and the chain of command responsible for advising the decision makers in the Line Chain (Staff Chain).

Combining this chart with organization charts* and written job descriptions for each of the personnel mentioned, results in making planned personnel requirements as accurate as possible, and creates a dynamic set of documents which form the basis of the company personnel acquisition policy during program implementation.

---

* Charts mentioned here are presented in the next section.

PERSONNEL ACQUISITION AND ORGANIZATION CHARTS

Codes

Job Function	Code
Board of Directors	BOD
President	P
Real-Estate Advisor	REA
Attorney	LLB
Accountant	CPA
Program Consultant	PC
Advertising Agency	AA
Architect-Interior Designer	AID
Banker	BNK
Prototype Manager	PM
Prototype Personnel	PP
Training Director	TD
Bookkeeper	BKP
Program Director	PD
Program Sales Manager	PSM
Purchasing Director	PD
Field Service Representatives	FSR
Advertising and Promotion Manager	APM
Program Salesmen	PS
General Counsel	GC
Staff and Research Assistant	SRA
Real-Estate Manager	REM
Marketing Director	MD
Controller	CON
Public Relations Manager	PRM

PERSONNEL ACQUISITION AND ORGANIZATION CHARTS

Exhibits 8.1 through 8.2 chart the schedules of the various stages of development of a new business (which we'll call the Unique Merchandising Company) and show the codes used in those charts. The organization charts that follow thereafter (Exhibits 8.3 through 8.7) show the development of the table of organization for the Company, by stages, until the last one, which

Exhibit 8.1: Projects

PROJECT	STAGE 1 Line Chain	STAGE 1 Staff Chain	STAGE 2 Line Chain	STAGE 2 Staff Chain	STAGE 3 Line Chain	STAGE 3 Staff Chain	STAGE 4 Line Chain	STAGE 4 Staff Chain	STAGE 5 Line Chain	STAGE 5 Staff Chain
1. Develop blueprint										
2. Select board of directors										
3. Arrange financing										
4. Establish corporation										
5. Determine advisors										
6. Select prototype site										
7. Design prototype and establish design criteria										
8. Select contractor for prototype										
9. Construct prototype										
10. Conduct prototype grand opening										
11. Develop operating manual										
12. Develop training manual										
13. Develop sales promotion package										
14. Develop program sales package										
15. Develop sales materials and operations package										
16. Develop accounting and control system										
17. Develop operator's agreement										
18. Develop newsletter										
19. Hire personnel: a) Prototype Manager b) Prototype Personnel c) Training Director d) Bookkeeper e) Program Director f) Program Sales Manager g) Purchasing Director h) Field Service Representatives i) Advertising and Promotion Manager j) Program Salesmen k) General Counsel l) Staff and Research Assistant m) Real-Estate Manager n) Marketing Director o) Controller p) Public Relations Manager										

PERSONNEL ACQUISITION AND ORGANIZATION CHARTS

Exhibit 8.2
Continuing Functions

FUNCTION	STAGE 1 Line Chain	STAGE 1 Staff Chain	STAGE 2 Line Chain	STAGE 2 Staff Chain	STAGE 3 Line Chain	STAGE 3 Staff Chain	STAGE 4 Line Chain	STAGE 4 Staff Chain	STAGE 5 Line Chain	STAGE 5 Staff Chain
Advertising										
Accounting/Control										
Finance										
Local Operator Sales										
Operator Field Support										
Local Operator Relations										
Site Selection										
Operator Training										
Legal										
Marketing										
Personnel										
Prototype Operations										
Public Relations										
Purchasing										
Research										
Sales Promotion										

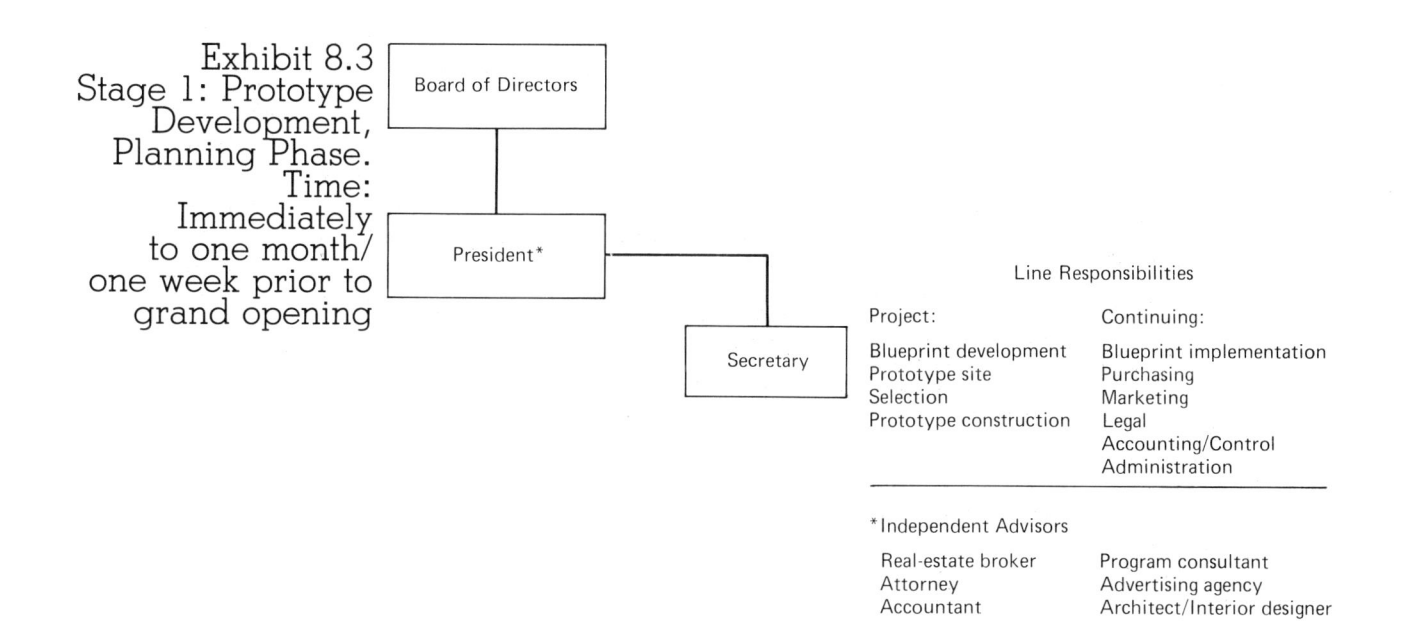

Exhibit 8.3
Stage 1: Prototype Development, Planning Phase.
Time: Immediately to one month/one week prior to grand opening

Board of Directors → President* → Secretary

Line Responsibilities

Project:
Blueprint development
Prototype site Selection
Prototype construction

Continuing:
Blueprint implementation
Purchasing
Marketing
Legal
Accounting/Control
Administration

*Independent Advisors

Real-estate broker
Attorney
Accountant

Program consultant
Advertising agency
Architect/Interior designer

REQUIRED ORGANIZATION PERSONNEL

**Exhibit 8.4
Stage 2: Prototype Development, Operational Phase.
Time: One month/one week prior to grand opening through six months of operations**

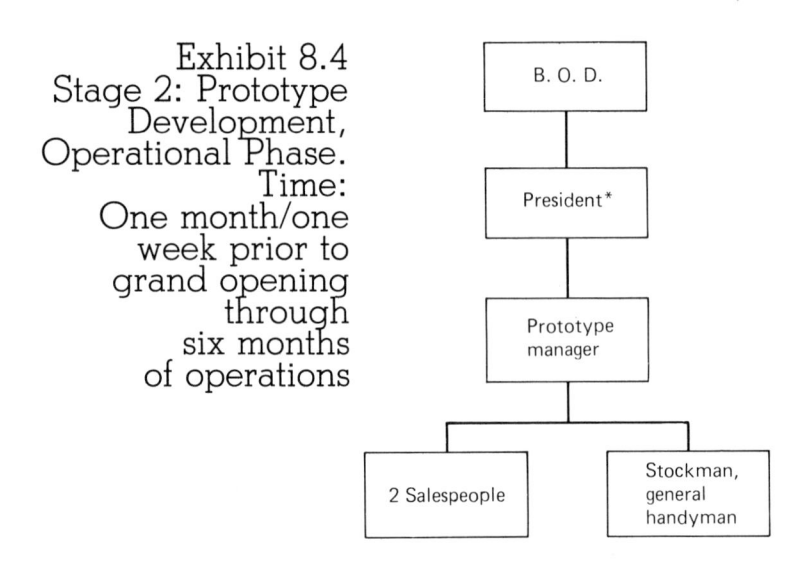

```
          B. O. D.
             |
         President*
             |
      Prototype manager
             |
      ┌──────┴──────┐
  2 Salespeople   Stockman,
                  general
                  handyman
```

*Independent Advisors

Attorney   Advertising agency
Accountant
Program consultant

N. B. Secretarial and clerical personnel to be added as required.

**Exhibit 8.5
Stage 3: Program Development.
Time: Six months after grand opening to one month prior to sale of first local business**

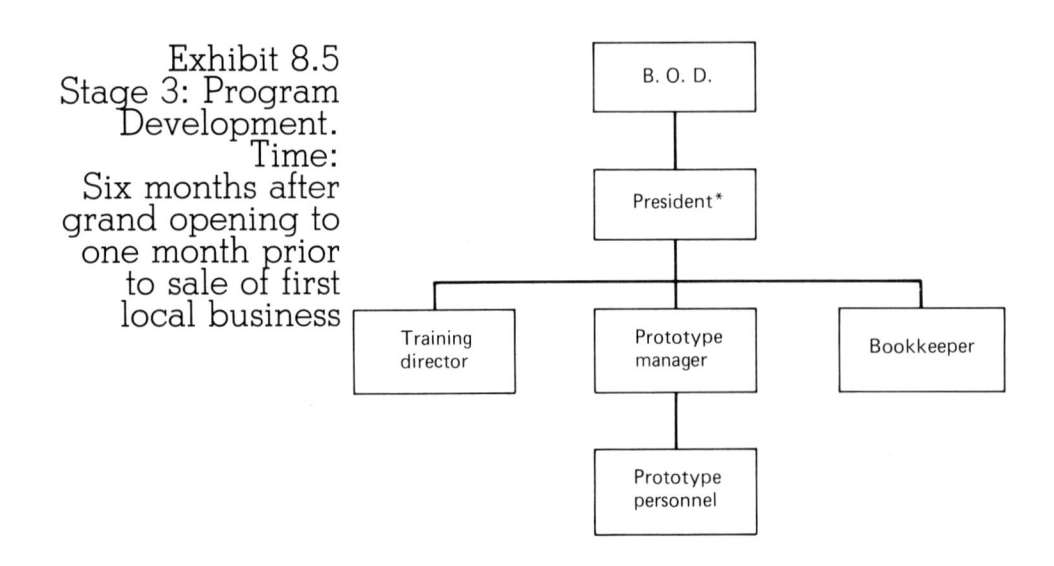

```
                B. O. D.
                   |
               President*
                   |
      ┌────────────┼────────────┐
  Training     Prototype     Bookkeeper
  director     manager
                   |
              Prototype
              personnel
```

*Independent Advisors

Attorney   Advertising agency
Accountant   Real-estate broker
Program consultant

N. B. Secretarial and clerical personnel to be added as required.

PERSONNEL ACQUISITION AND ORGANIZATION CHARTS

Exhibit 8.6: Stage 4; Sales and System Administration, Preparation. Time: One month prior to sale of first local business through sale of fifth one

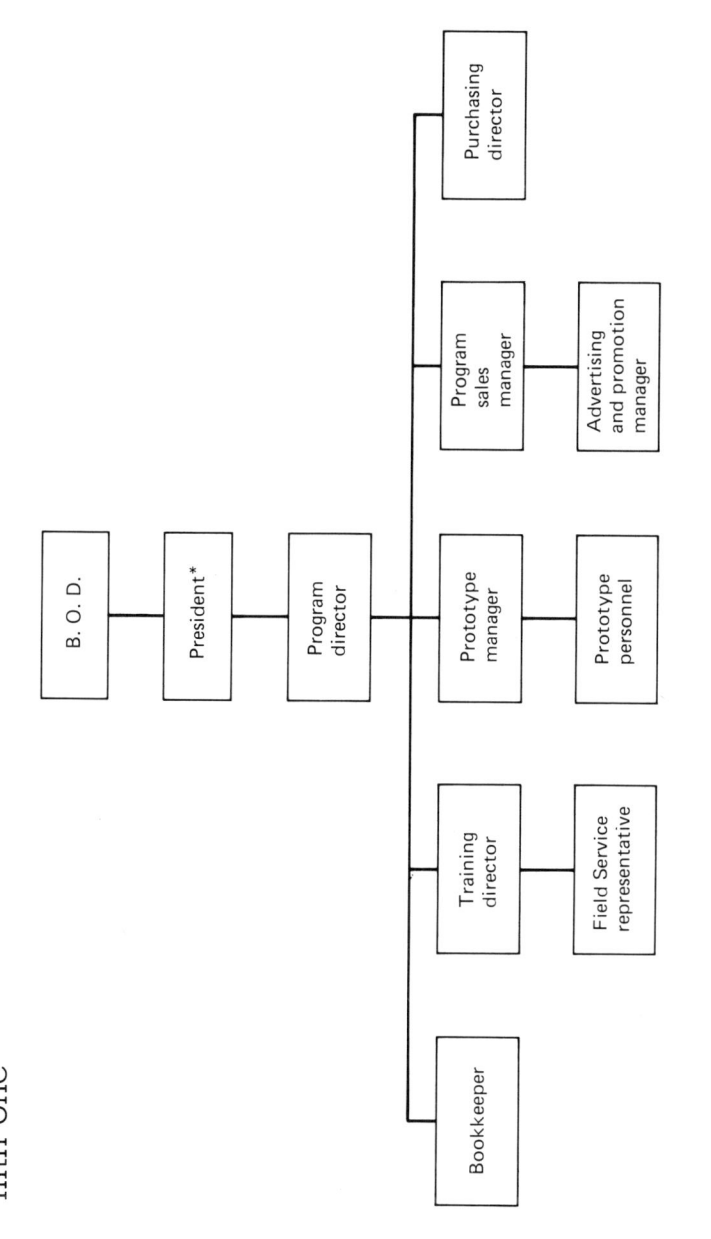

```
                          B. O. D.
                             |
                         President*
                             |
                     Program director
     _____|_____
     |            |              |              |             |
 Bookkeeper   Training       Prototype      Program        Purchasing
              director        manager         sales         director
                 |               |           manager
            Field Service    Prototype          |
            representative   personnel     Advertising
                                           and promotion
                                             manager
```

*Independent Advisors

Attorney   Advertising agency
Accountant   Real-estate broker
Program consultant

N. B. Secretarial and clerical personnel to be added as required

REQUIRED ORGANIZATION PERSONNEL

Exhibit 8.7: Stage 5; Sales and System Administration, Operation. Time: Concurrent with sale of fifth local business

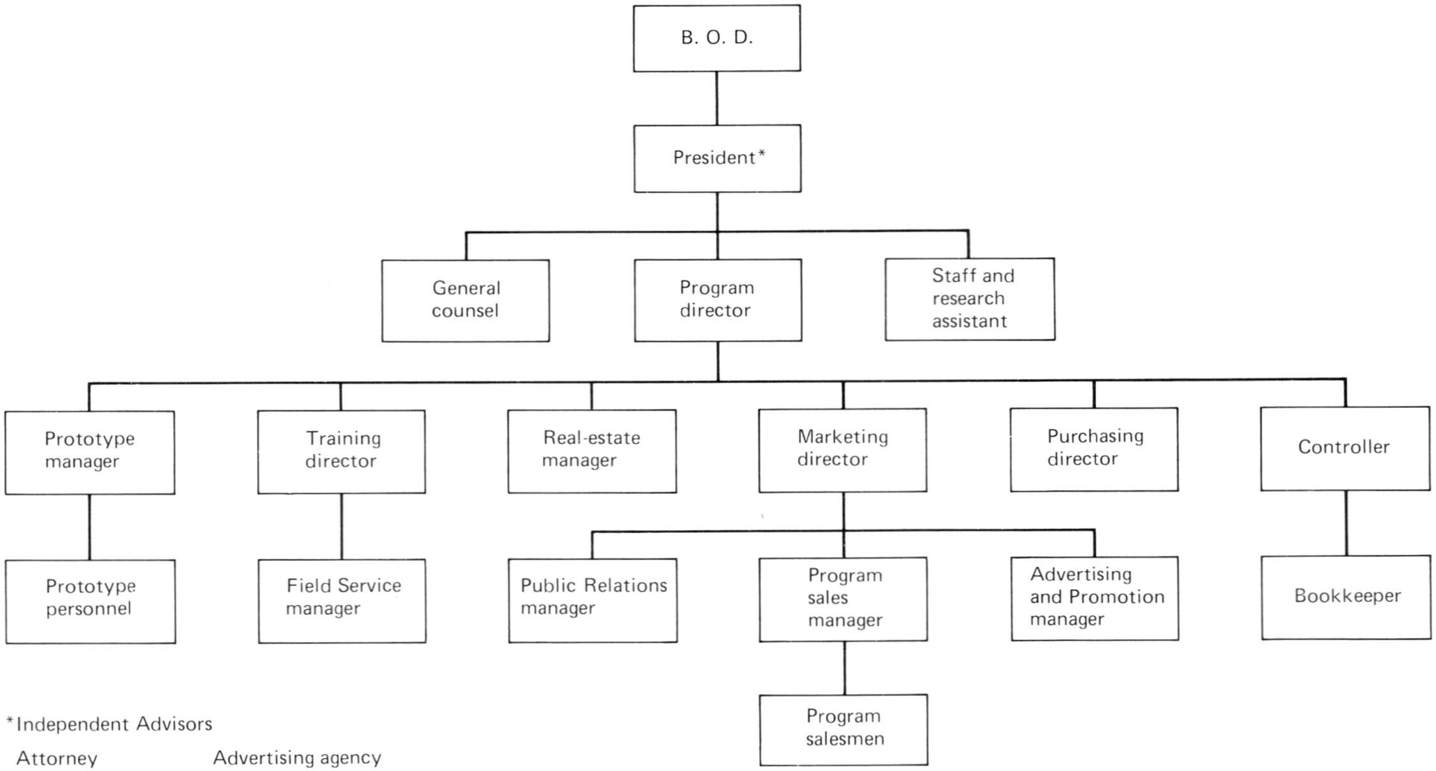

```
                                    B. O. D.
                                       |
                                   President*
                                       |
        ┌──────────────┬───────────────┼───────────────┬──────────────┐
     General        Program         Program         Staff and
     counsel        director        director        research
                                                    assistant
        
   ┌────────────┬──────────────┬──────────────┬──────────────┬──────────────┐
Prototype    Training      Real-estate    Marketing      Purchasing     Controller
manager      director      manager        director       director
   |            |              |              |                            |
Prototype    Field Service  Public         Program                      Bookkeeper
personnel    manager        Relations      sales
                            manager        manager
                                           |
                                        Program
                                        salesmen
                                           |
                                        Advertising
                                        and Promotion
                                        manager
```

*Independent Advisors

Attorney   Advertising agency
Accountant   Real-estate broker
Program consultant

N. B. Secretarial and clerical personnel to be added as required

gives a graphic view of the final operating organization by division and function. This is the Unique Merchandising Company's definitive Table of Organization.

EVALUATING JOB RESPONSIBILITIES

To provide additional details relative to the Table of Organization and personnel acquisitions, comments concerning the responsibilities and objectives of the various positions are in order.

MANPOWER SCHEDULING:

At the outset many of the duties charted in the Table of Organization will be conducted by a few persons. It is wise, however, to look ahead and to visualize the types of functions which will be needed at various growth stages and the types of personnel that may have to be acquired to handle these functions.

Job specifications are also defined to assure that there will be no overlapping of functions and commitments, and that each department has a clear-cut awareness of its basic day-by-day duties. Job specifications include:

▶ *Training:* During the initial stages, this should be conducted by the General Manager or Vice President of Operations and by the President. After recruitment of several operators, consideration should be given to the hiring of a *Training Director.*

▶ Designate a *Controller* within the second quarter. The necessity of financial controls becomes more evident as two local operators should have been recruited. As a result there will be need for close contact with the home office to keep control of expenditures. The Financial Department must become familiar with operations in the early stages of the overall program. During the initial stages of this program, an outside or part-time accountant could handle these functions. The part-time accountant would work closely with both the President and the Program Director to accumulate and tabulate data and to make necessary financial decisions.

▶ The *Advertising and Promotion Manager* and *Public Relations Manager* should be appointed after the twelfth month of operations. Grand openings will be taking place, which will mean considerable Public-Relations work. The proper development of sales promotions programs and pre-grand opening advertising programs is one of their functions. Initially this department can be handled by a qualified outside individual or company, until a full-time person may become economically necessary.

REQUIRED ORGANIZATION PERSONNEL

▶ Subsequent to the fifteenth month of operations, the *Manager of Field Services* should be added to the staff. It is anticipated that at the end of the fifteenth month of operations there might be 17 new local units, with at least eight new local businesses in full operation. Field situations will become apparent which will require competent solutions.

▶ During this same period of time (the fifteenth month), the *Purchasing Director* should be hired and become active. It is estimated that the local operators might be doing a combined volume of approximately $200,000 a month or $1,600,000 a year with 14 units in operation. This growth will require assistance in purchasing, and the Purchasing Director's job will become full-time by the fifteenth month of operations.

The preceding manpower scheduling is summarized as follows:

Manpower Scheduling Summary

Title	Appointment (after start of franchise sales)
President	1st month
Program Director	1st month
Program Manager	1st month
Secretary	1st month
Training Director	8th month
Controller	6th month
Advertising/Promotion Manager	7th month
Field Service Manager	13th month
Purchasing Director	15th month

Management Employees and Recommended Salaries to Start

	Suggested Salaries
President	Open
Program Sales Manager	Commission
Secretary	$10,000
Franchise Director	40,000
Training Director	20,000
Controller	25,000
Advertising, Sales Promotion, and Public-Relations Manager	35,000
Purchasing Director	18,000

TABLE OF ORGANIZATION

Those in management positions in the organization have many responsibilities both in common and individually.

Common Responsibilities

- To participate in the development of company policies and interpret these policies throughout the organization and to all local businesses.
- Develop objectives, policies and procedures for the organization, with the approval of directors.
- Interpret and administer programs and procedures for the organization, in accordance with approved policies.
- Develop expense budget objectives for the operation; require performance within budget.
- Develop a suitable successor and be responsible for training of such managerial replacements.
- Constantly evaluate the organizational plan, corporate objectives, manpower planning, and management appraisal, and budget controls as they relate to performance and goal accomplishments within the scope of company policies.
- Perform special assignments for superiors and function on special committees in accordance with the organization's needs.

INDIVIDUAL RESPONSIBILITIES

Position of Responsibility: President
Reporting Level: Board of Directors

Policy and Administrative Responsibilities:

- Develop corporate policies; interpret and administer.
- Develop corporate objectives, establishing achievement responsibilities for those objectives throughout the organization.
- Develop and approve corporate operating budgets which reflect plans and programs as related to corporate objectives.
- Train junior-level executives.
- Constantly evaluate corporate objectives in light of new developments.

REQUIRED ORGANIZATION PERSONNEL

Phasing: The President should assume executive duties as soon as possible and should be totally involved in the formative phases of the expansion program. The President should be completely aware of the needs and directions of the company and the local operators. The chief executive is responsible for establishing business policy and also has the major responsibility for carrying out these policies.

Position of Responsibility: Program Director
Reporting Level: Reports to President
Administrative and Managerial Duties:

- Coordinating all activities with the local operators.
- Final approval of site location with the advice of the Program Sales Manager.
- Layout planning and actual installation of furniture, fixtures, and equipment.
- Purchasing of all furniture, fixtures, and equipment.
- Providing assistance in the profitable, efficient utilization of all necessary materials.

Providing the Training function and working closely with the Training Director to accomplish the following:

- Recruit qualified personnel.
- Train the employees.
- Review Operations Training material and make recommendations for changes and improvements, stressing efficiency.
- Assist the Training Director in establishing training procedures when new products, methods, or promotional programs are developed.
- Frequent contact with each local operator, in person, or by phone or mail, in order to have a constant knowledge of the operational problems within the total organization.
- Preparation of the monthly operations reports on each local business for the President.

- ▶ Directing a Research and Development program to improve methods of providing services.
- ▶ Developing techniques for the efficient handling of inventory and control of inventory movement.
- ▶ Membership in the committee to evaluate local operator performance.
- ▶ Working with subordinate managers to solve problems of communications, administration, promotion, and supply before they reach crisis stage.
- ▶ Establishing the purchasing procedures for the operator in ordering the products.
- ▶ Planning of field operations, coordinating the various activities of the organization.
- ▶ Controlling incoming purchased materials, their inspection, and distribution.

Position of Responsibility: Secretary
Reporting Level: Reports directly to Program Director
Services: Program Director and others
Duties and Responsibilities:

- ▶ Handling the responses to all sales inquiries received.
- ▶ Transmitting prospect leads and material to the salesmen in the field.
- ▶ Maintaining files of the recruiting advertising analysis forms.
- ▶ Maintaining files on all potential prospects.
- ▶ Servicing the salesmen.
- ▶ Performing all duties as executive secretary and assistant to the Program Director.
- ▶ Arranging for the organization to receive status reports, as may be required from time to time.
- ▶ Establishing records and controls as required by the Program Director and staff.

REQUIRED ORGANIZATION PERSONNEL
100

Position of Responsibility: Purchasing Director
Reporting Level: Reports to Program Director
Administrative and Managerial Duties:

- Establishing and maintaining high quality product specifications.
- Locating alternative sources of supply for each product, which is purchased through the home office, in order to assure proper servicing of local businesses.
- Conducting an incoming inspection of all materials and products from vendors.
- Establishing warehousing facilities where need is evident. However, must make an all-out effort for the warehousing cost to be borne by local businesses or the vendor, wherever possible.
- Arranging product shipment and billing by vendor directly to local operator.
- Controlling product in accordance with the highest standards established by the home office.
- Purchasing analysis and evaluation as to product quality, price, sources available, delivery schedules, warehousing, discounting arrangements, and product damage or spoilage.
- Handling product distribution where product originates or is handled by the parent company.
- Establishing vendors and/or purchasing procedures from the home office for the local operators.

Position of Responsibility: Training Director
Reporting Level: Reports to Program Director
Administrative and Managerial Duties:

- Continuing development and administration of the training program.
- Supervising the home office training school as well as the training of the field and home office staff. Establishing procedures for hiring and administering all home office personnel.

- ▶ Making periodic visits to the local businesses to ascertain the effectiveness of the home office training program, as well as the effectiveness of the operator's training program for his or her employees.
- ▶ Assisting the local operators to develop their own staffs and to provide additional training materials for their use in the field.
- ▶ Revising or redeveloping training programs as indicated by experience and usage.
- ▶ Developing the techniques and systems for indoctrination of the local operators in any new programs which are created by the home office.
- ▶ Working closely with the Sales Director in the development of training materials and coordinating these materials with recruitment and public relations programs.
- ▶ Assisting in the development of material and techniques for Company regional and national meetings.

Position of Responsibility: Advertising/Promotion/Public-Relations Manager

Reporting Level: Reports to Marketing Director and Program Director

Administrative and Managerial Duties:

- ▶ Counselling and assisting in design and development of the marketing and merchandising programs for the local business network and the implementation thereafter.
- ▶ Working closely with the Field Service Manager in providing office support, maintenance of records relative to prospects, home office secretarial assistance, mailings and notifications, as well as other related sales support activities.
- ▶ Coordination and liaison of the recruitment program.
- ▶ Development and implementation of the advertising and sales promotion programs for both

REQUIRED ORGANIZATION PERSONNEL
102

the local business operations and the sales program.
- Conducting Public Relations programs for new units during the Grand Opening, as well as during operational phases.
- Establishing and maintaining national advertising budgets, schedules, and campaigns.
- Assisting and giving direction to the local operators in all areas of sales, merchandising, advertising, sales promotion, and public relations as such services are required in their local territories.
- Overseeing each operator's sales efforts and assisting in the development of the sales potential to its fullest capacity.
- Maintaining close contact with the local operators and observing their activities with an eye to improvement wherever possible.
- Working with operators in the field and helping in implementing the various promotional and merchandising programs designed to increase sales and profits.
- Assisting the operator organize his or her local advertising and sales promotion campaigns.
- Making monthly progress reports on sales and marketing activities of each local business, as well as a composit report for review by the Program Director.
- Being on the Committee to evaluate operator performance.
- Designing and developing various techniques, necessary for close communications with the operators on the state of the art in the industry as well as other new developments of importance.
- Pariticipating fully in the regional and national seminars to be held for the local businesses.

Position of Responsibility: Program Salesman

Duties and Responsibilities:

- ▶ Establishing qualification procedures and criteria which, in turn, must be consistant with the company's policies and objectives.
- ▶ Making a presentation to the potential operator, which presentation employs the skills of negative selling (a highly specialized technique generally required to sell intangibles).
- ▶ Negotiating all operator/company contracts with prospects and presenting all signed contracts, with the down-payment monies, to the Program Director for review and approval. Deriving compensation solely from commissions and defraying any normal expenses incurred during selling operations.

FIELD SUPERVISION

One of the key factors leading to the development of an enduring operator/company relationship will be the field supervision offered by the Field Service Manager for the successful operation of the network. It is the company's responsibility to provide Operations Personnel of the highest calibre to call on the local business for operational and supervisory purposes. The *initial* field supervision is of prime importance, since it will set the pace for the successful activity of the local business and its personnel. The initial field supervision should:

- ▶ Assist in the on-time completion of the local units.
- ▶ Help project the proper image to the community during the preopening stage.
- ▶ Assist in the hiring and training of the employee staff.
- ▶ Provide guidance and personal assistance in the implementation of the grand-opening promotion.
- ▶ Institute publicity and promotional programs and establish a continuing format to be adopted by the manager for exploitation.

After the initial field supervision, a program of continuing supervision must be instituted. The follow-up field supervision will not only serve to maintain the image set by the home office but will also serve to introduce new methods of operations and procedures, resulting in greater profits for the local operator. In addition, new ideas and promotions that may have been developed within the operating unit can be judged and worthy information sent to the entire network.

PERMITS AND LICENSES

In evaluating things to be done in establishing a new project, pertinent local regulations should be carefully considered. In some instances, local regulations may impose rigid constraints that can deter the commencement of the business for an inordinate period. In other instances—e.g., retail liquor stores, auto repair, restaurants—permits and licenses or special exemptions must be obtained which may drag on for months or may not be granted at all. Whatever the business to be established, all state and local regulations relevant to it must be thoroughly understood and planned for before any appreciable investment of time or money has been made.

CHAPTER NINE

OPTIONAL FORMS OF BUSINESS ORGANIZATION

OPTIONAL FORMS OF BUSINESS ORGANIZATION

Business organizations can take several different forms, each of which has its own advantages and disadvantages. A concept most common to all types of business organization is the limiting of losses to the business venture itself and the limiting of liabilities against the individual participants in the venture. Most successful experience has resulted from the use of the corporate form. Here liability for loss is limited to the investor's equity in the "legal individual" known as the corporation. However, there are other ways to do business and some are enumerated in the following pages, together with their own characteristics.

FRANCHISING

WHAT IS FRANCHISING? Franchising is a well-tested and proven method of accelerating market distribution which results in producing fees, royalty income, and new market penetration for the sponsor plus security and growth for the entrepreneurs. The franchisor provides the managerial expertise and the franchisees provide the distribution.

The traditional vertical chain of command has now evolved into a horizontal managerial relationship. Practical business considerations are responsible for this change to a marked degree, but franchise regulations now extant in fifteen states have also been influential.

STATUS OF FRANCHISING

Franchising continues to break new records in sales, employment, and number of establishments. Several factors have contributed to this phenomenal growth:

- ▶ New fields are being developed constantly for franchised operations.
- ▶ Foreign markets are being expanded.
- ▶ Franchisees are benefiting from the use of trade names, marketing expertise, acquisition of a distinctive business appearance, standardization of products and services, and advertising support by the parent organization.

In 1980, franchise sales of goods and services, according to a Department of Commerce study, are expected to exceed $280 billions, and the number of franchised establishments to exceed 468,000. Employment in franchising, including part-time workers and working proprietors, totals almost 4,000,000.

By merging local capital and energy with a national reputation, supervision, proven products, and the proven techniques of running such a business, an amalgamation is created whereby both parties are interested in the success of the business. If local franchisees are not successful, the manufacturer's program cannot succeed. If the manufacturer becomes lax or does not adapt to changing market conditions, the system of franchisees will falter. This mutually dependent relationship is believed to be responsible for the fewer failures in franchising than in other forms of retailing.

When the elements required for success in franchising are discussed, it must be remembered that the term franchising refers only to a system or channel of distribution. There are many other factors than the choice and utilization of a method of distribution which ultimately determines a firm's success or failure. Product quality, for example. If the product is unacceptable to the market for which it is intended, no distribution method will be able to deliver adequate sales. Also, other factors can be beyond the control of the firm. An enfranchised firm dependent, for example, upon the use of leased telephone lines to deliver its service cannot succeed if it is unable to secure access to those lines. Thus, when the determinants required for success in franchising are assessed, they must be considered from the all-other-factors-being-equal approach. Hence, franchising is not effective, per se, but only when a certain set of conditions prevail.

The franchisee is a local, independent businessperson who establishes a reputation and identity with the franchisor which is much closer than that of the usual independent "middleman." The franchisee is willing to submerge some of his or her personal identity because there are advantages to be obtained from the reputation and resources of a larger company.

Thus, it is observed that franchising is an arrangement whereby the franchisor, who has developed a successful product or service (plus a successful pattern or formula for the conduct of the particular kind of business), extends to franchisees the right, or privilege, of participating in that business as long as they follow the parent's established pattern or formula of operation.

OBLIGATIONS OF THE FRANCHISOR

In the usual franchise relationship, the franchisor provides the following to the franchisee:

- ▶ Use of the company trademark.
- ▶ Store location analysis and counsel. Assistance in purchase of site or negotiation of building lease.
- ▶ Assistance in the purchase of necessary initial equipment.

OPTIONAL FORMS OF BUSINESS ORGANIZATION

- Store construction or remodeling plans.
- Financial assistance in the form of a loan, allowing purchases on account, or countersigning loans obtained from a third party.
- Training of management and employees.
- Visit by field representative during the first week or more of pre-opening, opening, and grand-opening.
- Program of national advertising, publicity, and public relations.
- Merchandising assistance.
- Record keeping books and tax bulletins.
- Manual of operating procedures.
- On-the-spot field counseling on all aspects of conducting the business. Specialized home office counsel when required.
- Continual feedback of information on new developments.
- Savings through centralized purchasing.
- Preparation of materials for local advertising.

PARTNERSHIP CONCEPT

GENERAL PARTNERSHIPS A general partnership is an association of two or more individuals to operate a business for profit as co-owners. The major advantage is that double taxation is avoided, as there is no company income tax. The tax levy is paid by the individual partners.

The danger of this form of business organization is that each partner is fully liable, personally, for the debts of the partnership. This unlimited personal liability aspect of a partnership often mitigates against its use.

LIMITED PARTNERSHIP

A limited partnership has all the benefits of a general partnership but avoids the danger of unlimited liability for all partners. It is organized so that one of the group of partners has unlimited liability, just like a general partnership. However, the limited partner's liability is limited to only the amount invested in the partnership. The limited partner has no personal liability beyond his original investment. The limited partner may not participate in management and may not contribute services to the firm. The limited partner risks the loss of limited liability if he or she violates these provisions.

A *partnership* is a contract between two or more competent persons, to join together in business and to share the profits, each assuming unlimited liability for the affairs of the firm.

JOINT VENTURES

A joint venture can almost be regarded as a form of temporary partnership, unusual in the respect that it can be entered into by a corporation. Usually, a joint venture is an agreement between two or more persons to do some specific piece of business for a profit. Generally, the joint venture is limited to one transaction. Its origin is in antiquity when it was used to organize shipping ventures.

While a joint venture can be managed by all of those involved, it is more common to elect or appoint a syndicate manager, who acts as agent for all the others. When the purpose of the joint venture has been accomplished, the syndicate is dissolved and the profits or losses are apportioned according to the interests involved.

While joint venture agreements will vary substantially, according to the practices of the industry in which the agreement is operative, certain elements are common to all syndicate agreements. These are:

- ▶ Date, name and address of syndicate parties.
- ▶ Purpose of the joint venture.
- ▶ Amount of contribution by each syndicate member.
- ▶ Payment and amount contributed.
- ▶ Acquisition of property.

OPTIONAL FORMS OF BUSINESS ORGANIZATION
110

JOINT VENTURES

The joint venture, one of the oldest forms of business organization, is generally created for one specific piece of business and is terminated when the business is concluded. Participation is in relation to a prescribed interest and the business is conducted by a designated syndicate manager.

- ▶ Manner of holding title.
- ▶ Management of venture.
- ▶ Compensation of syndicate manager.
- ▶ Manager's indemnification.
- ▶ Liability of manager.
- ▶ Liability of participants.
- ▶ Division of profits.
- ▶ Payment of expenses.
- ▶ Payment of losses.
- ▶ Term of venture agreement.
- ▶ Arbitration of disputes.
- ▶ Interest payment on funds advanced.
- ▶ Deposit of funds.
- ▶ Default in payment of amount subscribed.
- ▶ Substitution of manager.
- ▶ Binding effect of manager's acts.
- ▶ Manner of giving notice.

- Subscribers not partners or agents.
- Binding effect of agreement.
- Leasing of business property.
- Termination or dissolution.
- Withdrawal of subscriber.
- Liquidation of business.
- Transfer of interest.

A company can expand by establishing one joint-venture arrangement—or a network of them—in which each party makes precommitments relative to functions and ownership participation. Joint venture arrangements vary greatly. Interests can be a majority type or a minority type.

CHAPTER TEN

ORGANIZING AN EFFECTIVE TRAINING PROGRAM

ORGANIZING AN EFFECTIVE TRAINING PROGRAM

The Blueprint should always provide for thorough training of the entrepreneurial manager. This is essential to help assure the smooth operation and eventual success of the business.

The training process should be practical, useful, and carefully structured. It should cover all basic parameters of the planned projects.

An important aspect of any training project is its operations manual. This is explained in detail in subsequent pages.

Also contained in this chapter are examples of training programs used by successful companies, and examples of operations manual preparations.

EVALUATION OF TRAINING NEEDS

IMPORTANCE OF TRAINING The essence of a successful expansion program and the base for all future attitudes at the local level—company loyalty, controlled drive, and implementation of the program—is established in the weeks the operator is under the direction of the home office for his or her initial training. It is during this short period of time that the groundwork for all future relationships is cemented and it is imperative that the time spent with the local operator during training is calculated to create the desired enthusiasm for the program, correct attitudes, will to succeed, and willingness to cooperate for the mutual advantage of all persons connected with the program. These attitudes must be formed along with the training of the operator and must be handled expertly. Along with the training that will enable the local owner to properly manage and operate the business must go the buildup of confidence that will make the owner sure that he or she has the ability to succeed.

The local operator must be convinced that operating this business is the opportunity to make a place in the community as an astute and successful business operator, rendering a needed service and making a profit while providing jobs and opportunities for others.

Attitudes leading to a success pattern are infused, not taught, during the training period and the selection of a training manager must be a careful and thoughtful process. The Training Manager must be a person who engenders confidence and rapport, respect and a desire to emulate. The Training Manager must be thoroughly versed in all operational aspects of the business—including personnel management, community relations, public relations, bookkeeping, housekeeping, inventory control, and customer service.

It must be assumed in this program, as in any other, that the local operator has no business background—and part of the training period must be devoted to the basic principles of business management, profit motives, and cost control. The unit operator must have a thorough understanding of business basics. Profit consists of those monies left over after *all* expenses are paid. A salary will be established for each owner based on minimum needs and will be considered an expense so that the true profit picture of any operation will be ingrained in the mind of the operator.

In this subject, as in all subjects taught in the training school, the Training Manager must teach in terms of basic education and must avoid the use of management, accounting, or trade "lingo." Classes must be short enough for complete absorption of the subject by the trainee, with enough time allotted to clear up any questions and resolve any doubts regarding a thorough understanding of the subject.

The first training period of the day will be the longest and will be devoted to a capsule revue of previously taught subjects—a quick question-and-answer period.

Since the mature owner-operator wants to get his or her unit to produce income as soon as possible, the training period away from that unit will be as short as is consistent with producing the necessary training results.

Three days of "school" training in a hotel, meeting hall, or studio room, and two days of "learn-by-doing" training in the prototype is recommended initially. Thereafter, an additional training period—e.g., one week—in the operator's own unit.

OPERATIONS MANUAL AS A VITAL TRAINING TOOL

An important tool in the training of the local operator is the Operations Manual. It should cover all of the necessary training areas in detail and should be designed to be used as a text during the training period at the home office. It should also serve as a permanent ready reference for the operator to give him or her the necessary guidelines for the proper operation of the business. It should cover the administrative aspects of the operation as well as the merchandising methods to be used for best results.

The entire Operations Manual should be specifically designed as a tool to be used in the functioning of the operator's business. It should be in loose-leaf form so that additions and deletions can be made as they become necessary and so that this "bible" can be kept up to date at all times, keeping pace with the changes in merchandising and promotion methods.

It should contain all needed procedures and other instruction. It should describe a complete personnel management program—from hiring employees to specific job qualifications and responsibilities. The Manual should contain specific information on all subjects covered in the training period, in addition to promotional material for the local operator's use.

A TENTATIVE OUTLINE FOR A STORE OPERATIONS MANUAL

Section A
Introduction
- Foreword
- Company history
- The people behind you
- Company's obligation to you
- Operator's obligation

Section B
Pre-opening procedures
- Time-table, from agreement to grand opening
- Receiving fixtures and inventory
- Obtaining advisory services
- Obtaining insurance program
- Obtaining licenses and permits
- Obtaining utilities and other services
- Trade publications and reference books suggested
- Checklists of actions to take:
  - three to four months before opening
  - two to three months before opening
  - one to two months before opening
  - Within 30 days before opening

Section C
Store policies
- Image
- Quality standards of products
- Price policy
- Brand policy
- Service and courtesy
- Delivery to customers
- Customer credit
- Check cashing
- Complaints and refunds
- Guarantees
- Maintenance
- Relationship with community
- Store hours
- Employee discounts

Section D
Store routine and housekeeping
- General housekeeping
- Basic duties of personnel: store manager, clerks, etc.
- Daily store-opening procedure—checklists
- Daily store-closing procedure—checklists

OPERATIONS MANUAL AS A VITAL TRAINING TOOL
117

                              Checking out register and daily report
                              Maintenance of store and equipment
                              Self-inspection

▶ **Section E**   Order-taking procedure (writing up order)
Sales Routine   Operating cash register
                              Making change
                              Sales taxes
                              Charge-account procedure (if applicable)
                              Mail-order procedure (if applicable)
                              Exchanges, adjustments, refunds (procedure)
                              Bags and packages
                              Want book

▶ **Section F**   Initial orders, showing supply source and initial
    Supplies   quantity (by category and item)
and inventory   Purchase order forms—how to use for new orders
                              Checking in shipments
                              Payment
                              Pricing procedures
                              Taking inventory—procedure and forms
                              Inventory control and order planning guide: form
                              showing minimum quantities (item by item); how
                              much to build to when minimum is reached, etc.
                              Preventing losses (through poor records, pilferage,
                              shoplifting)

▶ **Section G**   Personnel
Administration   Job chart
                                  Hiring, qualifications, interviewing
                                  Application form, checking references
                                  Hours, shifts, timekeeping
                                  Vacations, sick pay, time off
                                  Employee discounts
                                  Payroll taxes, laws concerning employees
                                  Rules of conduct for employees
                                  Training
                              Field supervisor's inspection

ORGANIZING AN EFFECTIVE TRAINING PROGRAM

                              Communications and reports (forms to use)
                                  Between stores and home office
                                  Between stores and warehouse
                                  Recurring reports to home office
                              Record-keeping and accounting

▶ **Section H**   Grand opening promotion plans with timetable
Sales promotion   General promotion
                                Newspaper, radio, direct mail
                              Seasonal events, major holidays, etc.
                              Display

A TABLE OF CONTENTS FOR AN OPERATIONS MANUAL FOR A SERVICE-TYPE BUSINESS

A—Policy

Policy
Response to inquiries
Telephone sales
Customer contacts
Handling customer complaints
Use of equipment
Servicing and maintenance of equipment
Customer follow-up
Spare parts
Van
Uniform
Credit cards
Your relationship with community

B—Operations, Procedures

Job procedures—sequence of steps
Planning your work
Surveying the job to be done
Estimating procedure
    Job estimate and customer order form
    Work order and invoice form
    Estimating instructions
Customer's checklist
Performing the job—operator's checklist
    Verifying starting time
    Checking and servicing equipment
    Time report

Greeting customer
Erecting lawn sign
Customer checklist
Accident prevention
Inspection
Customer acceptance
Collecting payment

C—Lead development, promotion, and selling

Prospects and lead development
  What is a "lead"?
  Who are your prospects?
  Where do your leads come from?
  Prospect status card
  Customer referral incentive plan
  Promotion at the job site
  Door hanger invitation
Budgeting and planning your advertising
  Co-op advertising
Yellow pages advertising
Newspaper advertising
  Types and example of ads
  How to mark proofs
Direct mail and literature
  Direct mailer
  Reply card
  Literature
  Literature samples
Radio and television
  Radio spots
Counter cards
  "Take one" insert card
Publicity and public relations
Customer relations
  Sample literature
Selling
  Sales brochure
Mechanics of the sale
  Basic steps
  Selling recap

SELF-INSPECTION CHECKLIST

Name _____ Store No. _____

Location _____ Date _____

	Store Exterior	Yes	No
1	Sidewalk clean		
2	Sidewalk in good repair		
3	Window—glass clean		
4	Window—proper signs		
5	Window—proper size lights		
6	Window—lights operating		
7	Window—base below clean		
8	Sign clean		
9	Sign lighted		
10	Entrance clean		
11	Doors in good condition		
12	Awning clean		
13	Awning in good repair		
14	Building walls in good repair		
15	Building walls clean		
16	Grassy area neat		
17	Rear of store neat		
18	Trash containers good condition		
19	Trash containers in place		
20			
21			
22			

	Store Interior—Front	Yes	No
23	Floor clean		
24	Ceiling in good condition		
25	Walls in good condition		
26	Fixtures in good condition		
27	Lights proper size		
28	All lights working		
29	Lights clean		
30	Phone booth clean		
31	Directory in good condition (if not, order new one)		
32	Weighing scales clean		
33	Weighing scales accurate		
34	Stamp machines operating		
35	Glass in cases clean		
36	Area behind counters clean		
37	Trash containers in place		
38			
39			
40			
41			
42			
43			
44			

OPERATIONS MANUAL AS A VITAL TRAINING TOOL

	MERCHANDISE DEPARTMENTS	a Stock Clean Yes / No	b Stock in Order Yes / No	c Stock Priced Yes / No	d Any out of Date Yes / No	e Shelves Filled Yes / No	f Compulsory Display Use Yes / No	g Discontinued Mdse. Yes / No	h Yes / No
45	Proprietary								
46	Toiletries								
47	Cosmetics								
48	Baby								
49	Sundries								
50	Ice cream								
51	Candy/Gum								
52	Tobacco								
53	Housewares								
54	Hardware								
55	Pet supplies								
56	Greeting cards								
57	School supplies								
58	Magazines/books								
59	Convalescent								
60	Photo supplies								
61									
62									
63									
64									
65									

ORGANIZING AN EFFECTIVE TRAINING PROGRAM

Prescription Department		Yes	No
66	Stock clean		
67	Stock in order		
68	Drawer mdse. in order		
69	Outdated-unsaleable mdse. pulled		
70	Scales & weights clean		
71	Prescriptions double-checked and signed		
72	Narcotic prescript. canceled		
73	All restricted drugs dispensed by registered pharmacist		
74	Proper utensils on hand		
75	Utensils in proper condition		
76	Narcotic cabinet locked		
77	Prescription records in order		
78	Prescription files in order		
79	Sale of poisons recorded		
80	Sale of narcotics recorded		
81	Poison control emergency phone #		
82	Reference books in place		
83	Containers and bottles neat		
84	Containers and bottles in sufficient supply, right sizes		
85	Refrigerator in order		
86	Proper items under refrigeration		
87			
88			
89			

Storage & Supplies in Reserve		Yes	No
90	Mdse. stock neatly arranged		
91	Arranged by dept.		
92	Items of same category together in same place		
93	Trash containers in place		
94	Floor clean		
95	Packaging supplies neat		
96	Packaging supplies sufficient		
97	Supply of forms sufficient		
98	Cleaning supplies neat		
99	Cleaning supplies sufficient		
100	Reserve register tape rolls		
101	Lighting sufficient		
102			
103			
104			
105			
106			
107			
108			

Personnel		Yes	No
109	Neatly dressed		
110	Clean jackets		
111	Clean shaven, neat haircuts		
112	Clean hands & fingernails		
113	Good customer approach		
114	Courtesy		
115	Familiar with mdse.		
116	Lost sales recorded		
117	Know regular customer names		
118	Proper register procedure		
119	Proper change making		
120	Interest in work		
121	Smoking habits controlled		
122	Personal phone calls controlled		
123			
124			
125			
126			
127			
128			
129			

General		Yes	No
130	Bulletins & checklists posted		
131	Charge acct. procedure followed		
132	Fire extinguishers renewed and in proper places		
133	Register receipts legible		
134	Photo work (developing) kept orderly		
135	Photo work record kept		
136	Store licenses & certificates posted prominently		
137	Cigar humidor working & filled		
138	Air conditioning ok		
139	Wrapping, bagging material on hand in right places		
140	Displays & price signs clean		
141	Emergency phone numbers at hand		
142			
143			
144			
145			
146			
147			

Washroom		Yes	No
148	Floor clean		
149	Ceiling, walls clean		
150	Lighting sufficient		
151	Mirror clean		
152	Basin clean		
153	Toilet bowl clean		
154	Towels in place		
155	Soap sufficient		
156	Toilet paper & spare roll		
157	Waste receptacle		
158	Door lock in order		
159			
160			
161			
162			

Instructions:
1. *When used by operators for self-inspection.* Make notes of deficiencies on reverse side of this sheet. Identify each comment by line number corresponding to the item. Retain for your own use as a check on correction of deficiencies noted.

2. *When used by field supervisors.* Sign and attach this form to Field Supervisor's Inspection Report form. It then becomes part of your report.

Field Supervisor's Signature _____

Form #

OPERATOR TRAINING CURRICULUM AND SCHEDULE OF CLASSES

SUNDAY (or one day prior to first session)

Operator arrives at home-office city and checks into hotel accommodations provided. If operator and spouse are to undergo training program together, the Company will provide double room accommodation. If the operator will undergo training alone, then single accommodations will be provided.

When the trainee checks into the hotel there should be a letter for him or her at the desk, stating exactly (1) when and where the first meeting will be held and (2) when and where transportation (if needed) will be provided.

The Training Director should call hotel during the evening to ascertain that the operator has arrived.

FIRST DAY (Monday)

Time and Instructor	Subject
8:30 A.M. Training Director	*Official Greetings* (As trainees enter, each receives a copy of this schedule and a pad and pencil in a Kraft envelope.) Introduction of trainees to each other. Introduction of all executive personnel involved in various company functions, such as: ▶ Administration ▶ Controller ▶ Supplies (Inventory) ▶ Field Supervision ▶ Other top executives
9:00 A.M.	*Welcoming Speech by President*

ORGANIZING AN EFFECTIVE TRAINING PROGRAM

9:30 A.M.   *The Parent Company*

(name)   Background, history, etc. Reasons for establishment of company. Need for personal service, etc. Aims. Philosophy of operation. The Company creed.

10:00 A.M.   *Coffee Break*

10:30 A.M.   *Headquarters Tour*

Guided tour through various company divisions, with head of each division acting as host—giving brief description of activities.

Noon   *Lunch*

1:00 P.M.   *Tour of Company Warehouse and Distribution Facilities*
Observation of order-filling process, shipping, etc.

3:15 P.M.   *Coffee Break*
Return to classroom

3:30 P.M.   *Distribution of Operations Manual*

3:45 P.M.   *Subject: "Pre-opening Procedures"*

(Name)
- Fixtures and Inventory
- Advisory services
- Insurance program
- Licenses and permits
- Utilities and other services
- Checklists for phases of timetable
- Trade associations
- Early publicity

(to be continued tomorrow)

5:00 P.M.   *Questions and Answers* pertaining to material covered so far

5:30 P.M.   *Dismissal*

6:30 P.M.   *Dinner*

OPERATOR TRAINING CURRICULUM AND SCHEDULE OF CLASSES

SECOND DAY (Tuesday)

8:30 A.M.	*Questions and Answers* relating to previous day's subjects
9:00 A.M. (name)	*"Pre-opening Procedures"* continued (See subjects on preceding page)
10:00 A.M.	*Coffee Break*
10:30 A.M. (name)	*"Pre-opening Procedures"* continued
Noon	*Lunch*
1:00 P.M.	*Visit to Prototype Operation* (Have coffee break prior to returning to classroom)
3:00 P.M. (name)	*Subject: "Personnel Requirements"* ▶ Job chart ▶ Job descriptions and qualifications ▶ Sources of personnel ▶ Hiring and interviewing ▶ Employee benefits
4:00 P.M. (name)	*Subject: "Store Policies"* ▶ Image ▶ Brands ▶ Prices ▶ Customer service and complaints. Delivery. ▶ Charge accounts, checks, etc. ▶ Maintenance ▶ Relationship with community
5:00 P.M.	*Questions and Answers*
5:30 P.M.	*Dismissal*
6:30 P.M.	*Dinner*

THIRD DAY (Wednesday)

8:30 A.M.	*Questions and Answers* relating to previous day's subjects
9:00 A.M. (name)	*Subject: "Store Routine"* ▶ Basic duties of personnel and owner ▶ Store opening and closing procedures ▶ Housekeeping and Maintenance ▶ Self-Inspection
10:00 A.M.	*Coffee Break*
10:30 A.M.	*"Store Routine" continued*
Noon	*Lunch*
1:00 P.M. (name)	*Subject: "Sales Activity"* ▶ Servicing customers ▶ Ringing up sales—operating register ▶ Collecting payment—cash, checks, etc. ▶ Charge account procedure ▶ Bagging ▶ Want Book
3:00 P.M.	*Coffee Break*
3:30 P.M.	*"Sales Activity" continued*
5:00 P.M.	*Questions and Answers*
5:30 P.M.	*Dismissal*
6:30 P.M.	*Dinner*

FOURTH DAY (Thursday)

8:30 A.M.	*Questions and Answers* relating to previous day's subjects
9:00 A.M. (name)	*Subject: "Merchandise Plan and Inventory System"* ▶ Basic merchandise plan ▶ Inventory maintenance and control

	▶ Turnover
	▶ Inventory maintenance procedure
	▶ Mechanics of ordering
	▶ Receiving and checking
	▶ Price labeling
10:00 A.M.	*Coffee Break*
10:30 A.M.	*"Inventory System" continued*
Noon	*Lunch*
1:00 P.M.	*"Inventory System" continued*
3:00 P.M.	*Coffee Break*
3:30 P.M.	*"Inventory System" continued*
5:00 P.M.	*Questions and Answers*
5:30 P.M.	*Dismissal*
6:30 P.M.	*Dinner*

FIFTH DAY (Friday)

8:30 A.M.	*Questions and Answers* relating to previous day's subjects
9:00 A.M. (name)	*Subject: "Store Routine"*
	▶ Core of the company image
	▶ Persons authorized in area
	▶ Inventory and control
	▶ Layout of area
	▶ Routine for filling orders
	▶ Packaging, labeling
	▶ Pricing
	▶ Licenses and permits
10:00 A.M.	*Coffee Break*
10:30 A.M.	*"Store Routine" continued*
Noon	*Lunch*
1:00 P.M.	*"Store Routine" continued*
3:00 P.M.	*Coffee Break*

ORGANIZING AN EFFECTIVE TRAINING PROGRAM

3:30 P.M.	*Questions and Answers*
5:00 P.M.	*Dismissal*
6:30 P.M.	*Dinner*

SIXTH DAY (Saturday)

8:30 A.M.	*Questions and Answers* relating to previous day's subjects
9:00 A.M.	*Subject: "Administration"*
(name)	▶ Personnel: 　▶ Hours, shifts, etc. 　▶ Rules of conduct 　▶ Discount 　▶ Evaluation 　▶ Training ▶ Store security ▶ Field supervisor's inspection ▶ Communications and reports ▶ Store supplies
10:00 A.M.	*Coffee Break*
10:30 A.M.	*"Administration" continued*
Noon	*Lunch*
1:00 P.M.	*"Administration" continued*
(name)	▶ Retail pricing ▶ Accounts receivable procedure ▶ Accounting system and record keeping
3:00 P.M.	*Coffee Break*
3:30 P.M.	*"Administration" continued*
5:00 P.M.	*Questions and Answers*
5:30 P.M.	*Dismissal*
6:30 P.M.	*Dinner*

SEVENTH DAY (Sunday)

Day of rest and relaxation

EIGHTH DAY (Monday)

8:30 A.M. — *Questions and Answers* relating to previous session's subjects

9:00 A.M. — *Subject: "Employee Training"*

(name)

- ▶ Methods of training and place
- ▶ Extent of training
- ▶ Scheduling
- ▶ Training tools
- ▶ Follow-up with supervision
- ▶ Training curriculum
- ▶ Salesmanship training

10:00 A.M. — *Coffee Break*

10:30 A.M. — *"Employee Training" continued*

Noon — *Lunch*

1:00 P.M. — *Subject: "Sales Promotion"*

(name)

- ▶ Grand opening
  - ▶ Events and ceremonies
  - ▶ Pre-view
  - ▶ Promotional ideas, door prizes, etc.
  - ▶ Media
  - ▶ Time table and checklist
  - ▶ Newspaper ads, radio, publicity
- ▶ Future promotion
  - ▶ Newspaper
  - ▶ Publicity
  - ▶ Radio
  - ▶ Direct mail

ORGANIZING AN EFFECTIVE TRAINING PROGRAM

        ▶ Planning calendar—seasonal promotions
        ▶ Display

3:00 P.M.	*Coffee Break*
3:30 P.M.	*"Sales Promotion" continued*
5:00 P.M.	*Questions and Answers*
5:30 P.M.	*Dismissal*
6:30 P.M.	*Dinner*

NINTH DAY (Tuesday)

8:30 A.M.	*Questions and Answers* relating to previous day's subjects
9:00 A.M. (name)	*Review of All Training Subjects*
10:00 A.M.	*Coffee Break*
10:20 A.M.	*Review continued*
Noon	*Lunch*
1:00 P.M.	*Review continued*
3:00 P.M.	*Coffee Break*
3:30 P.M.	*Review continued*
5:00 P.M.	*Dismissal*
6:30 P.M.	*Cocktail Party and Farewell Dinner*

TENTH DAY (Wednesday)

9:00 A.M.	*Operations Complete Report* Each operator trainee fills out training program report form, regarding effectiveness of training, indicating areas where more information is

	needed. These are analyzed by training staff before 10:30 period.
10:15 A.M.	*Coffee Break*
10:30 A.M.	*Individual and Group Consultation*
(All instructors on hand)	Weak areas indicated by operators are cleared up with further attention by appropriate instructors.
Noon	*Lunch*
(With President & executives	
1:30 P.M.	*Consultations continued*
2:30 P.M.	*Dismissal* (optional) All executive personnel will be on hand at this time to meet with any operators who feel the need for individual consultation or further explanations. Operators not requiring this are free to depart at their convenience.

The preceding formal training is to be followed by one week in field. Whether this week should follow the training immediately or at a later time has to be decided in advance by the home office.

BEN FRANKLIN FOUR-WEEK NEW-STORE-OWNER TRAINING SCHEDULE

Most Ben Franklin franchisees have retailing experience and, in fact, the greatest majority of them have variety store background. More than one half of new Ben Franklin franchisees are former chain store managers and, therefore, have a rich background in variety store retailing. All we need to teach them is the Ben Franklin Program and Systems.

To accomplish this, each new store owner attends a four-week training session at one of approximately 20 training stores around the country. These stores are owned and operated by individual franchisees who voluntarily give their time to train new owners under actual everyday operating conditions. Training costs are included in the franchisee's initial investment for his new store.

In addition to the attached program for in-store training, all new franchisees also spend three days in any one of eight of our regional offices for indoctrination.

First Week: Checking, Ordering, and Receiving Procedures

Completed (Please Check)

▶ *First Day—Welcome and Introduction* to all store personnel. Pull the organization together for a brief meeting, emphasizing that it is an honor to have _____ with them for four weeks, an honor to be the store selected to serve as the trainee store for assisting _____ to do a better job in his or her new store.

_____

At this time briefly explain the four-week training program.

_____

Spend time reviewing in-store activity on sales floor and general operation of the store with tour of each department observing merchandise assortment. (The new owner's daily work schedule should be the same as the owner in whose store the training is being given.)

_____

Review of all Check List books.

_____

At the end of each day the new owner should make a list of things he or she may not have completely understood that day. The next day should begin with a brief review for clarification.

▶ *Second Day—Stockroom:* Spend a full day receiving/checking freight. (Should be on the day a Ben Franklin warehouse order is received.)

_____

Indoctrination of freight book and its relationship to the operation. Enter the day's shipments.

_____

Proper pricing procedure, marking merchandise, dating style goods, advantages of using new pre-printed price labels.

_____

Tour of stockroom, covering proper layout, stock alignment.

_____

Protection of merchandise against *soilage* and *pilferage, security, claim area, supplies, fixtures, lay-*

BEN FRANKLIN TRAINING SCHEDULE

                                                          Completed

aways, seasonal carryover. (All these key points will be covered individually over the next four-week period.) _____

▶ *Third and Fourth Days—Merchandising:* Complete review of checklist books, on the sales floor, with the sales person in each department; study of layouts and checklist diagrams, association of key items to display; review of droplist items, SMS and new items added. _____

Review of basic factory and seasonal listings. _____

It is important here to assign a specific person to handle each area during these two (2) days.

▶ *Fifth and Sixth Days:* Check and order entire departments using E.O.S. (On store's transmitting day, actually handle transmitting procedure of an order. It is important here to assign a specific person to handle this area.) _____

Bin I.D. Tickets _____

Analyze Item Activity Report. _____

Cover and order SMS items. _____

Reorder of seasonal items. _____

Order of regular and Deal E factory orders. _____

Second Week: Operations

▶ *First Day—Office Procedure:* Learn the system and procedures with actual participation of daily cash and sales report. (Supplement cash office forms attached),* _____

---

* In an actual training program, these and other forms cited later would be attached to this schedule.

ORGANIZING AN EFFECTIVE TRAINING PROGRAM

Completed

Register procedure: Actual read-out of registers; use of forms; over and short; employee purchases; state and local taxes; lay-away payment follow-through; handling of cash procedure for any vending machines; rental Blue Lustre machines; other concessions; etc. _____

Correct handling of sale coupons. _____

Review of open order file. _____

Actual working invoices and claims. _____

▶ *Second Day:* Learn and work the following systems and procedures:

Open to buy (sample form attached) _____
Cash flow (maximum $1,000 on hand—to be covered by insurance) _____
Markups _____
Markdowns _____
Payroll _____
Set up of cash fund _____
Personnel scheduling (worksheet attached) _____
Checkbook handling _____
Bank reconciliation form _____
Payment of expense items _____

Review employee benefits and policies such as sick pay, vacation, insurance, review increases, etc. (guideline supplement attached). _____

▶ *Third Day:* Step-by-step review of:

P & L statement _____
Merchandise register _____
Operating budget (Frank Discussion of early danger signals and corrective measures to take. Budget should be reviewed 90 days after opening for possible revision by owner and Retail Sales Manager.) _____

	Completed
Expense register	_____
Supplemental work sheet on effects of promotions to staples (example attached) plus work sheet to actually work out.	_____
Review of all operating forms and function of each.	_____
Inventory—Correct procedure for taking inventory (supplement guidelines attached). Inventory control and protection of inventory.	_____

▶ *Fourth Day:* Participate in the actual handling of the daily cash routine:

Charge cards	_____
Payment of the statement terms	_____
Special dating of merchandise	_____
Relationship between the statement and the freight-receiving Book	_____
Actual checking off of the statement	_____

▶ *Fifth Day:* The following should be reviewed again:

Daily cash routine	_____
Seasonal code information on invoices	_____
Ben Franklin mailing check-off	_____
A review of the first two weeks with free time for areas that need further discussion.	_____

▶ *Sixth Day:* Home

Third Week: Sales Promotion and Profit

▶ *First Day:* At this time the Retail Sales Manager should be in the store and actually work and review the new owner's advertising budget

Completed

and advertising and promotional plans with him or her. As much information as possible should be available to the trainee/owner on the town in which he or she is locating, advertising costs, newspaper distribution, circular cost distribution, etc.

Learn and set up advertising budget. _____
Learn to set up a six-week advertising plan, item selection from monthly sale plan, monthly promotional offerings, basic and seasonal checklists, etc. _____
Learn setting up of promotional and advertising file, correct handling of slicks, mats and sale-plan advertising materials. _____
Poster service _____

▶ *Second Day:* Learn end counter profit and productivity control, one-item ends, high-gross ends, seasonal impact ends, low-gross week-end promotions (always maintaining basic-staple assortment once customer is in the store to offset low-gross promotions), permanent basic-staple ends (Ex.: G.E. light bulbs), participate in making advance end plans and working on floor with department sales personnel. (Use floor plan form attached.) _____

Set up a twelve-month merchandise promotional file. _____

▶ *Third Day:* Use employee training film. If employees of trainee store have not seen this film, arrange their schedules before-hand so they can do so at this time. (Training film will be made available to the store by the Retail Sales Manager.) _____
Conduct weekly employee meeting _____
Merchandise turnover and how to figure _____
Seasonal record-keeping _____
Advance seasonal buying _____
Quarterly-return-sheet buying _____

BEN FRANKLIN TRAINING SCHEDULE

Completed

▶ *Fourth Day:* Complete and thorough discussion of gross profit, shrinkage control, and Ben Franklin's role as a partner to make the store prosperous. _____

Review special services (supplement forms and information sheets attached):

Advertising   Ad mat _____
Poster service _____

Merchandise   Garden seeds _____
Greeting card racks _____
Notion racks _____
General order program _____

General services   Retail accounting* _____
Electronic ordering system _____
I.D. tickets _____
Preprinted price labels _____
Item activity report _____

How to handle authorized reps calling on stores. _____

Proper handling of will-follow items and cancellations; handling of weekly price changes. _____

Chicago Pool shipments and ordering procedure; Timex watches, Matchbox cars. _____

Over-the-counter warranty; return procedures. _____

Handling of late factory orders; proper follow-up procedure. _____

▶ *Fifth Day:* A visit from the Retail Sales Manager to cover all of his or her functions and responsibilities and how it all relates between stores, region, and headquarters (regional-headquarters organization flow charts attached); a review of what the owner has covered in the first three weeks and answering any questions he or she may have; purpose and use of Regional/National Advisory Board.

---

*Full review with Retail Accounting Manager, 4th week, 4th day.

ORGANIZING AN EFFECTIVE TRAINING PROGRAM

Completed

▶ *Sixth Day:* Check and place store's weekly orders:

E.O.S. checklist _____
Seasonal _____
Sale plan _____

Actually handle transmission of orders, adjusting this schedule to transmitting day, if necessary. _____

Visual checking of key factory sources for replacement orders. _____

Saturday week-end traffic check; observe personal service, checkout performance, handle cash pickups, bank deposit. _____

Fourth Week

▶ *First Day:* A half-day visit from Apparel Coordinator and a half-day visit from Fabric/Homecraft Coordinator; review of Coordinator's specific areas, merchandise offerings, record keeping, return sheets, factory follow-up procedure. _____

Importance of attending spring/fall merchandise shows. _____

Apparel Coordinator (outline of things to be covered attached). _____

Fabric/Homecraft Coordinator (outline of things to be covered attached). _____

▶ *Second Day:* Review of stockroom and office procedures (including the Occupation-Safety-Health Act requirements—copy of OSHA from the state of new owner's location will be made available); actually participate in handling of daily cash, checking or making entries; briefly review Weeks 1, 2, and 3, especially areas that need further explanation. _____

Completed

▶ *Third Day:* Review the preopening of a new store. (If a Ben Franklin store is opening in the immediate area during this four-week orientation period, this schedule should be adjusted so a visit can be made.) At this time review only the store being visited. Do not get into the trainee/owner's preopening. This will be handled by the Retail Sales Manager in detail.

This should include merchandise-fixture planning, merchandising procedure, manager's role in store opening, employee hiring, scheduling, training, payroll control, advertising, preplanning after opening, promotional and advertising program.   _____

▶ *Fourth Day:* A visit from the Retail Accounting Manager, with a full discussion of Ben Franklin retail accounting procedures.   _____

▶ *Fifth Day:* An open review covering the four-week indoctrination.   _____

Fifth Week

New owner will be scheduled to revisit the regional distribution center prior to going into his or her store.   _____

CHAPTER ELEVEN

EFFECTIVE
PROGRAM
IMPLEMENTATION

OPERATOR SUPERVISION BY HOME OFFICE

Physical follow-up and backup by the home office is important in order to assure maximum operator accomplishment. This is necessary to supplement the mail and telephone sales procedures, and should be done on a regular, systematic, prescheduled basis.

At various intervals, personal visits should be made by either or all of the following members of the parent company: (a) Sales Manager; (b) President or Vice President; (c) Field Service Supervisor. The effect of such visits should be:

- Trouble-shooting to ascertain problems that have impeded the local operator's progress—or have caused recurring objections and complaints from customers—and to help solve them.
- Sales backup—to help the operator overcome sales difficulties due to inadequacies in such factors as Approach, Presentation, Close, Meeting Objections, etc.
- Service backup—this acts to: (a) help the local business solve current service problems; (b) help the operator obtain a current "big job" through assistance in his or her installation and estimating problems; (c) accompany operator to installations about which customers have complained to help eliminate these difficulties. To retain operator in service factors (mechanism, installation specifications, estimating, etc.), in order to help at the "roots" of the local business requirements.

SUPERVISION VIA MUTUAL ASSISTANCE

National organizations have found it highly effective to enlist the assistance of "stronger" local operators to help back up "weaker" situations. Often operators may not be completely responsive to advice and assistance from the home office, interpreting such efforts as theoretical or prejudiced, and slanted toward home-office objectives more than toward local objectives. Hence, there is value in assigning a successful operator to help an unsuccessful business. A kindred spirit is engendered. One operator respects and trusts the other's recommendations because both have similar objectives. The theory prevails that "You can't argue with success." Hence, if the helping operator is successful, the instructions are more readily absorbed.

Organizations accomplish such mutual help programs through:

- ▶ Setting up a "big-brother" status among operators.
- ▶ Arranging for operators in contiguous territories to help.
- ▶ Setting up regional territory operations with the regional business being in supervision of member local operators within the area.
- ▶ Home-office territorial supervisors.

BIG BROTHER STATUS

Under this plan, key operators in each area—selected on the basis of their experience, proven accomplishments—and a given number of local businesses in nearby areas (usually four to seven) are organized into an informal group. As "big brother," the key operator is available to advise member businesses and to help solve recurring problems. Thus, a localized tight-knit nucleus has been established for continuing guidance. The home office should establish an instruction program for these "big brothers" in methods for such instruction and guidance. A reward plan should also be established by the home office, so that such "big brothers" would benefit in proportion to the improved results they achieve.

ADJOINING TERRITORIES

Local operators receive encouragement from the knowledge that they can talk out their problems with other operators in adjoining areas. This gives them a sense of belonging to a large family, and helps their attitude and pride toward their work.

Sponsoring organizations set up the mechanics to enable adjoining territorial operators to get together—to feel free to contact each other as the need arises. One sponsor in the closed-circuit television field arranged a "working together" approach with the local businesses, enlisting the technical strength of one operator (who was weak in sales) and the sales strength of another operator (who was weak in technical aspects) to help each other and thereby complement each other's weaknesses.

REGIONAL CLINICS

This plan is in wide use with many sponsoring organizations and has proven highly effective. At regular intervals (usually monthly or bimonthly) operators in adjoining territories meet in a central location—thus constituting a regional clinic. The meetings are presided over by the most successful local operator in that area (for example, the "big-brother" type previously described) or by a representative of the home office (usually the Sales Manager). Objectives of such clinics are to provide a forum for an interchange of common business problems and the methods of solving them.

HOME-OFFICE SUPERVISORS

Such individuals become roving ambassadors of the sponsoring organization, assisting local operators with their problems and, in addition, encouraging them in their endeavors. Their functions include: (a) examining the operator's books and activity records to ascertain what is wrong and in which areas improvement is indicated; (b) counseling the local operator in sales or service problems; (c) achieving an improved bridge between the local businesses and the home office; (d) helping operators to improve relations with customers.

SUMMARY

The effect of everything stated here is to alert sponsoring companies to the importance of continuing guidance of their local operators. To the extent that this is achieved, to a maximum degree, the sponsoring organization will enjoy maximum success. The organization that has experienced failure in its programming is generally one that has lacked good contact with its local businesses, with its operators becoming just so many separated, semi-hostile units rather than satisfied, cohesive members of a large close-knit family.

Proper supervision of local operators:

- ▶ Builds morale.
- ▶ Decentralizes home-office functions.
- ▶ Permits regional control and follow-up.
- ▶ Achieves constant channels for communication between the parent organization and the local operator.
- ▶ Assures maximum morale on the part of the operator.
- ▶ Gives operators a winning momentum during the first six months of their operation—normally the critical period for the new business since it is the period during which they are most likely to fail if they are not properly and closely supervised and backed up.

EXAMPLES OF SUPPORT SERVICES

Continuing Support Services to Operators

GENERAL BUSINESS SERVICES, INC.

▶ *Materials and Supplies:* All materials and supplies needed either by the operator or his clients are provided and the Systems Development Committee improvements are ongoing. Over three-hundred items available are listed in the Operations Manual.

▶ *Operations Manual:* All volumes of the confidential Operations Manual are provided each field director. The know-how of many experts and years of experience by local operators provide proven programs and techniques. Changes to the volumes of the Operations Manuals are made as needed, and it is the responsibility of the Field Director to study and incorporate the new material promptly. The manuals are held in the custody of the Field Director but remain the property of Business Services, Inc. and *must* be returned upon request.

▶ *Tax Research Department:* The Tax Advisory Service is a no-charge unique program to assist Field Directors and their registered clients with income tax problems on a year-round basis. Also available from the Research Department is the Tax Research Service for attorneys.

▶ *Return Preparation Service:* This service, backed by the BSI guarantee of accuracy, relieves the operator from becoming a tax expert and preparing client income tax returns.

▶ *Tax Bulletin Service:* Each registered BSI client receives monthly the *Washington Alert*. Each month each Field Director receives three copies, enclosed with a newsletter, which offer tax-saving ideas and business management information specifically for owners of small businesses.

▶ *Training:* The monthly meetings of the region, the expanded regional meetings, and the two tax seminars each year provide ongoing training that contributes to the operator's professional development.

▶ *Lending Library:* Local operators can check out books, tapes, and other material to aid their professional development.

▶ *Promotional Efforts:* Promotional efforts on a continuing basis enhance the BSI image and are designed to help operators obtain clients and be quickly identified with the BSI trademark in local communities.

▶ *Computer Services:* Computerized Bookkeeping Service is a time-saving, efficient and accurate record keeping method for more complex clients. The accounts-receivable program helps clients collect from customers.

▶ *Sales Service:* A list of territories for sale is regularly sent to Regional Directors to help operators who wish to sell their businesses.

▶ *Monthly Billing Service:* Operators may have clients billed monthly by the national office and thereby avoid becoming collection agents.

▶ *Field Services:* Technical guidance on handling particular clients and transactions is available. In addition, professional staff members are available on a special assignment (per diem) basis to help operators in personal visits with clients.

▶ *Personal Insurance Programs:* Six insurance coverages, including Professional Liability, are available on a group basis.

▶ *Regional Directors:* In addition to training and counseling, Regional Directors coordinate many promotional and other activities within a region to benefit the group. The Regional Director also handles liaison with state and local governments to learn about new rules and regulations; this saves the individual operator time and effort.

▶ *National Account Program:* Contacts with national organizations help operators to both sell and service more clients.

▶ *Governmental Affairs:* The increasing number of state and federal laws and regulations involving tax preparers, etc., are monitored.

▶ *Approved Vendor Sources:* Suppliers who will provide quality products or services to operators, at substantial savings, are selected and listed in the Operations Manual.

▶ *Research and Development:* The national office coordinates the research and development of new products and services. Individual operators, through pilot programs, also test new products and services. This allows a local operator to quickly learn if a new product or service has already been investigated.

▶ *Financial Assistance:* To help solve a cash-flow problem, operators may take advantage of the service contract replacement plan under the monthly billing service. Collection of notes from the sale of territorial rights can be processed through the national office. Use of credit cards is also available. Loans through the Small Business Administration or banks are more easily obtained when a BSI business is involved than when individuals are on their own.

▶ *Other Support:* Four divisional Vice Presidents work closely with Regional Directors to help operators increase client registrations and improve their operations. The President's Advisory Council provides important input to the Management Committee of BSI. One of the most important benefits of being a BSI operator is the informal support and help from neighboring businesses—on a continuing basis and particularly in time of crisis.

CHAPTER TWELVE

EVALUATING TIMING AND COORDINATION REQUIREMENTS

PERT TECHNIQUE

ORIGINS OF PERT CHARTS During World War II, the United States Department of the Navy worked in conjunction with the consulting firm of Booze-Allen-Hamilton in developing a control technique which came to be known as PERT, an acronym for *Project Evaluation and Review Technique*. Later, this technique was expanded and more precise uses for it defined, and it became known as PERT-CPM, or *Project Evaluation and Review Technique—Critical Path Method*. Although both PERT and PERT-CPM were conceived and developed in response to a need for greater control and efficiency in the construction of naval vessels, it was soon found that they had broad applications in many areas. More sophisticated members of the business community applied them to a variety of problems, projects, and programs—ranging from coordinated sales efforts, to product manufacture, to plant construction, to new venture formation and implementation, to personnel scheduling.

While PERT-CPM represents a subject with a great many ramifications and consequent complexities, the basic technique is so important and useful that any blueprint that does not avail itself of it can probably be considered to be incomplete.

PERT CHART FUNDAMENTALS

Essentially, PERT-CPM calls for the statement, in the form of a chart, of events which must occur in order that a certain and specified goal be achieved. The events themselves are related to each other both by their position on the graph and by lines connecting them. Position specifies relative chronology; that is, it tells *when* an event must occur in relation to other events that are connected to it by lines. Lines specify the precise order in which events must occur.

A RESTAURANT COMPANY'S PERT-CPM

As an example, Company A, a restaurant company, is operating profitably in a local market and has developed menu items, food service techniques, decor, and promotion which its officers believe will be equally successful in additional local markets. Studies and research have confirmed this opinion. The decision has been reached to embark on a program of expansion, the first step of which will be opening and operating a restaurant in an area which has been determined to be suitable for Company A's operation. Company A's officers and management wish to utilize PERT-CPM as a planning and control technique to accomplish this end.

A RESTAURANT COMPANY'S PERT-CPM

PERT CHART DEVELOPMENT

Every PERT-CPM chart must have its beginning and its end. The beginning must be the situation as it exists on the day it is drawn, and the end must be the specific goal whose attainment is sought. In the case of the Department of the Navy during World War II, the beginning was usually the existence of a set of blueprints for a vessel and a predetermination of the yard at which it was to be built. The end was the launching of the vessel and the fondly held hope that it would float. In the present case, the beginning is the existence of a successful restaurant and the predetermination of a general area in which it is to be duplicated in its more important aspects. The end is the grand opening of that essentially duplicated restaurant and the fondly held hope that it, too, will "float."

In its simplest terms, then, a PERT chart can be drawn as in Exhibit 12.1.

While this simple diagram does not convey much information or allow the exertion of much control, it does serve the purpose of defining, very precisely, that construction on the restaurant must commence prior to its being completed, and that the restaurant must be completed prior to its grand opening. The block marked "Grand opening" follows the block marked "Complete restaurant construction," and that block follows the block marked "Commence restaurant construction"—thus *position defines the relative chronology of those events that are connected by lines*. The lines lead from "Commence restaurant construction" to "Complete restaurant construction" and hence to "grand opening"—thus *lines specify the precise order in which the events must occur*.

More useful—and perhaps sufficient for some purposes when considered as a part of an overall program (but still not sufficient for the purposes of Company A's officers and management)—is the PERT chart in Exhibit 12.2. Time is now specified, and once the commencement of construction is fixed with respect to a date, then a person—the Chairman of the Board of Directors of Company A, as an example—will know when he or she can begin activities that have been planned and that presuppose or are contingent upon the opening of the restaurant in question. In fact, with respect to those activi-

Exhibit 12.1

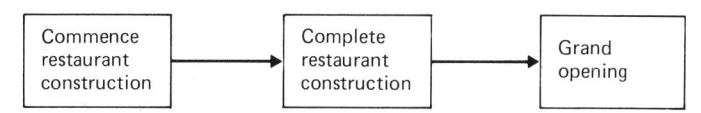

Commence restaurant construction → Complete restaurant construction → Grand opening

EVALUATING TIMING AND COORDINATION REQUIREMENTS

Exhibit 12.2

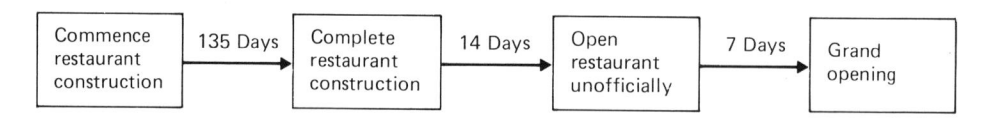

```
[Commence restaurant construction] --135 Days--> [Complete restaurant construction] --14 Days--> [Open restaurant unofficially] --7 Days--> [Grand opening]
```

ties, this example together with the assignment of dates may be all that is required or even desired.

The officers and management of Company A who are directly concerned with the details that go into the construction and opening of that restaurant, however, are concerned with—and require—far more information to function effectively. As an example, they must see to it that the best possible site within the given general area is chosen, and that the best possible terms for acquisition of the site are arranged. Even more useful, for their purposes, then, is the PERT chart shown in Exhibit 12.3. Of course, many more events must occur and many more functions must be performed before the restaurant may be opened. Company A must apply for and obtain all permits and licenses pertinent to constructing and operating a restaurant business at the selected location, it must arrange for equipment to be delivered and installed, it must arrange for hiring and training personnel, and a plethora of additional activities and events must take place in order that the specified goal—"grand opening"—may take place. Many of these events are not interdependent in themselves, although "grand opening" depends on the completion of each of them. Some events may take place concurrently. In fact, in order that the goal be attained within the stated parameter of six months, some events *must* take place concurrently. Exhibit 12.4 shows Company A's developed PERT-CPM chart.

Exhibit 12.3

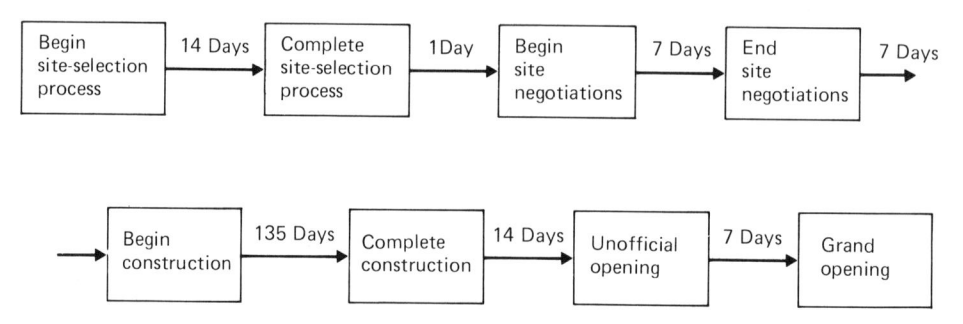

```
[Begin site-selection process] --14 Days--> [Complete site-selection process] --1 Day--> [Begin site negotiations] --7 Days--> [End site negotiations] --7 Days-->

--> [Begin construction] --135 Days--> [Complete construction] --14 Days--> [Unofficial opening] --7 Days--> [Grand opening]
```

Exhibit 12.4: Company A PERT–CPM Chart

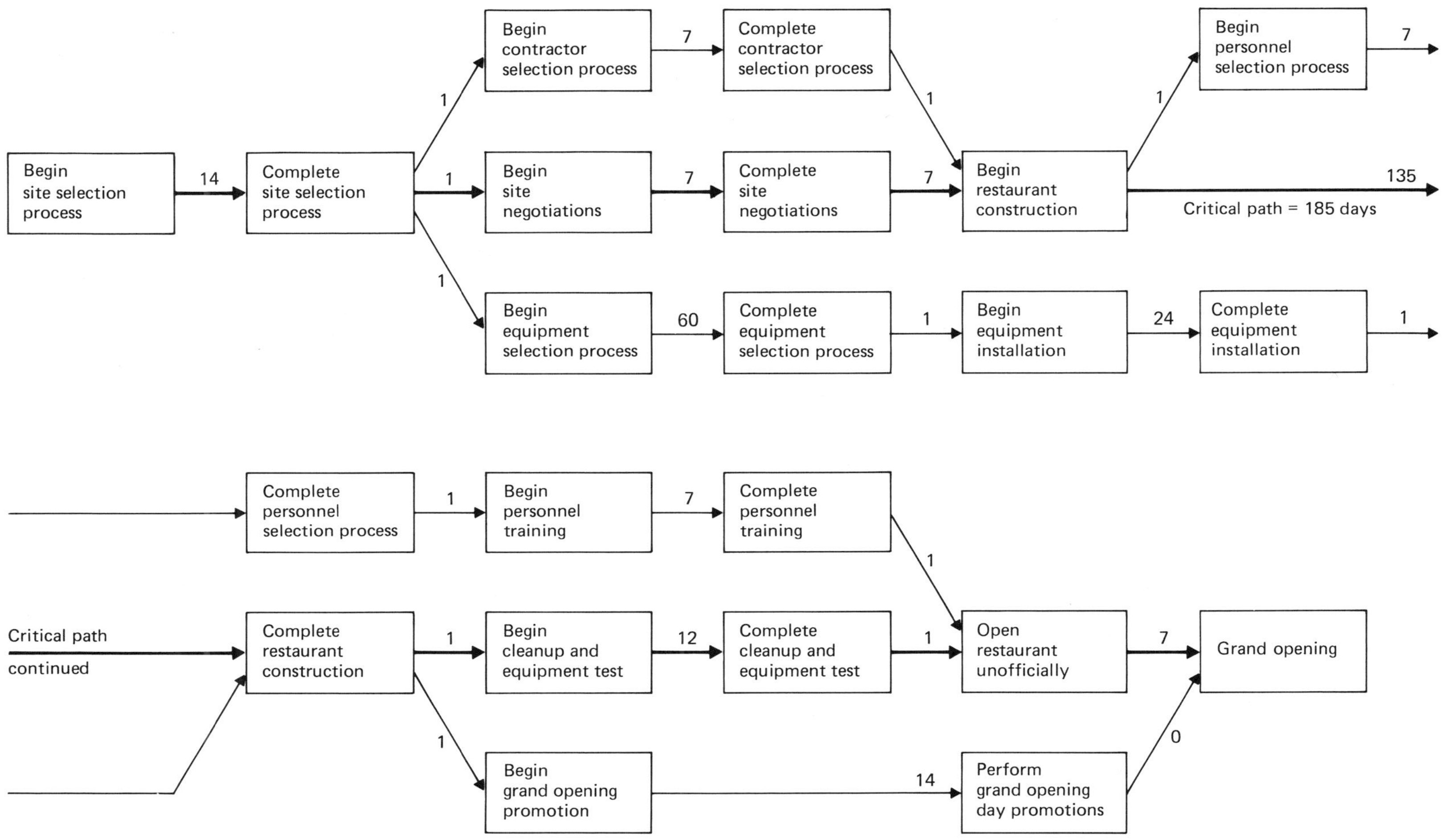

DEFINING THE CRITICAL PATH

The chart in Exhibit 12.4 is still not complete in every detail—the entire licensing procedure must still be added, for example—but its use as a planning and control tool may now be visualized with facility. Furthermore, it is now possible to define a "critical path," the CPM part of PERT-CPM. To accomplish this, the time periods associated with each interdependent event are summed, from the present to the attainment of the desired event. Starting with "Begin site selection process" and summing the days in the path from that point "Grand opening," we have: 14 + 1 + 7 + 7 + 135 + 1 + 12 + 1 + 7 = 185.

Going from start to finish by way of the "Begin equipment selection process" branch yields 122 days; by way of the "Begin contractor selection process" path it's 179 days; by way of "Begin personnel selection process" it's 53 days; and by way of "Begin grand opening promotion" it's 179 days. The path exhibiting the greatest sum—185 days in this case—is the "critical path," and "Grand opening" may be scheduled to take place 185 days from the beginning of the site selection process. Further, the contractor selection process must begin a maximum of 185 − 179 = 6 days after the commencement of the project. Otherwise, the critical path will be affected and the grand opening will be delayed beyond its projected date—perhaps at great cost and inconvenience. The same procedure may be followed with respect to each of the other defined paths to obtain specific starting dates for each of the subprojects which make up the total project.

PERT IMPLEMENTATION BENEFITS

As the project proceeds, the officers and management of Company A are able to control and administer it with far better knowledge of the cost and the time implications of variance from plan than they could without the use of PERT-CPM. As an example, an unforeseen delay in construction immediately indicates the need for canceling and rescheduling media space that may have been obtained for the promotion of the grand opening.

PERT CHARTS FOR SUBPROJECTS

It should also be noted that the time between "Begin restaurant construction" and "Complete restaurant construction" must necessarily contain a large number of interrelated and interdependent events. The critical path for this time span has been found to be 135 days, but that time may be further subdivided and a PERT chart and critical path developed for the construction process. Work on electrical wiring and flooring may be carried out concurrently, for instance, but equipment may not be installed and tested till the electrical work is completed and the flooring is laid. Consequently, it is to be hoped that Company A's management will insist on the selected contractor's developing a PERT-CPM chart for the project's construction phase.

Thus it may be seen that PERT-CPM technique has a vital and necessary place in any properly developed blueprint. As a planning tool it is unparalleled for efficiency, and its use during program implementation permits judgements and assessments to be made with maximum accuracy. In fact, when considered together with a complete set of projections as described in the "Arithmetic" section of this book, PERT-CPM may be considered as a detailed blueprint of the program.

ANCILLARY BENEFITS OF PERT

As with financial projections, one of the most valuable functions performed by application of PERT-CPM technique also is one of the least obvious. The finished chart or charts are extremely useful, but in addition to this obvious fact it is virtually impossible to overstate the value of the work which leads to their production. The format of the charts in themselves forces discipline. If they are to be complete and to serve fully the purposes for which they are intended, the individual or group responsible for their preparation *must* comprehend the planned project or program thoroughly, not only in overall concept, but in detail. In a surprisingly large percentage of instances, it has been noted that (1) the person preparing a PERT-CPM has called upon other members of the organization for advice and for the information required to complete the charts and that (2) the ensuing dialogue has served to increase the understanding of both parties relevant to the functions, problems, goals, organizational position, and importance of the party providing that information. In light of the organizational benefits, working efficiency, and spirit of cooperation which usually results, this sort of exchange should be encouraged at every opportunity and at every level. Exhibit 12.5, on the next page, is a flow chart that has been developed for use in a franchising industry, and its careful study is recommended. The following section shows the combination of PERT-CPM technique with checklists at critical points in a program's development.

PERT-CPM SCHEDULING

As will be noted from an examination of Company A's PERT-CPM that was developed in large part in Exhibit 12.4, and as has been stated earlier, PERT-CPM technique specifies relative chronology. However, specifying absolute chronology—scheduling and controlling the subprojects that combine to form the overall project—is usually more clearly and precisely accomplished by altering the PERT-CPM format. Thus Exhibit 12.6, on pages 160 and 161, is

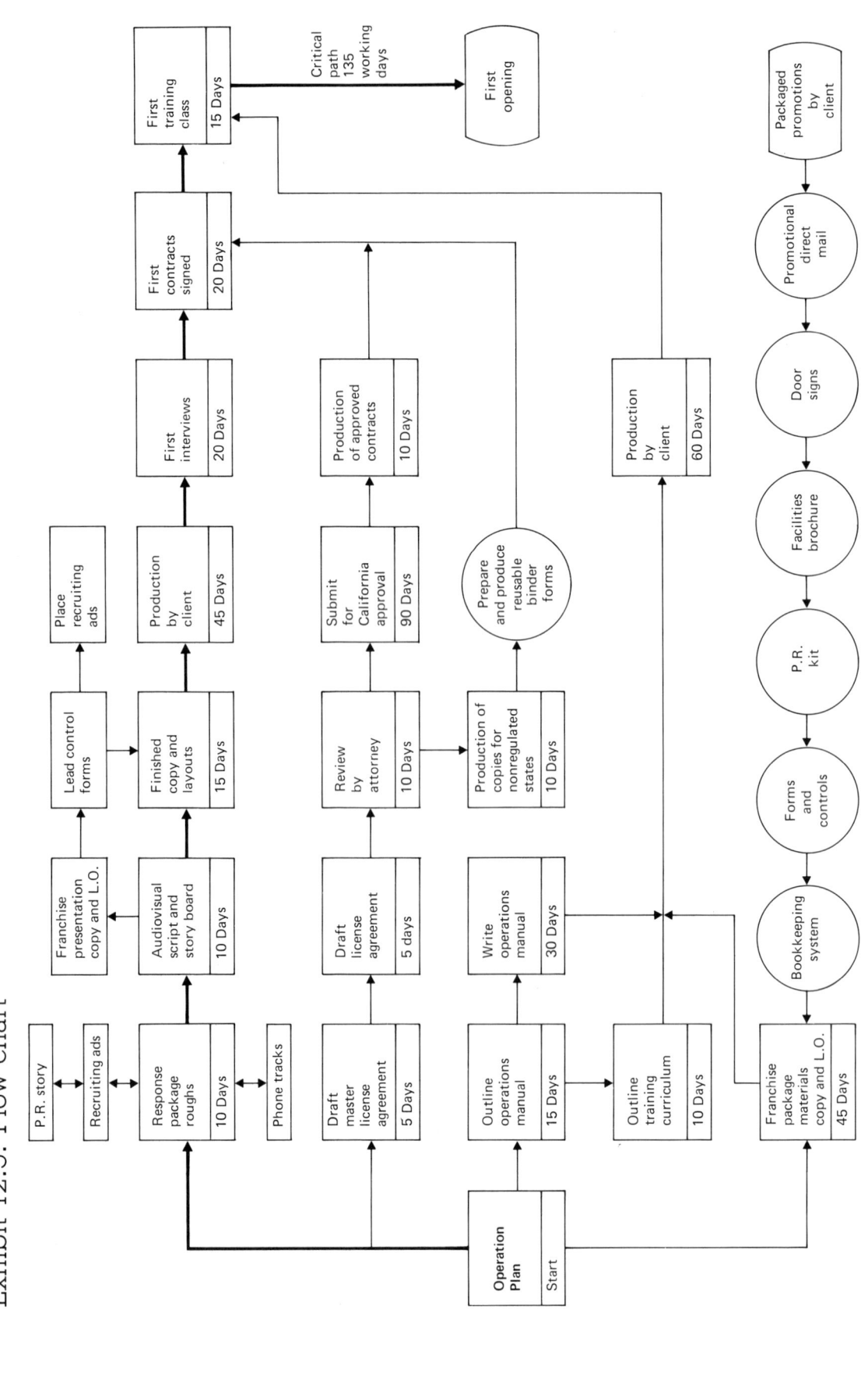

Exhibit 12.5: Flow chart

divided into "Critical Path Subprojects" and "Noncritical Path Subprojects." The chart's horizontal axis depicts each day of the overall program, from day 1, the beginning of the project, to day 185, the restaurant's grand opening. Each subproject is blocked out on the chart, and the key shows how to distinguish between "Critical Path Subprojects" and "Noncritical Path Subprojects."

It will be noted that "Critical Path Subprojects" extend through every day of the program with one exception: Days 23 through 28, inclusive, are blank. This time period will be utilized as a combination of safety factor and for site preparation prior to the commencement of construction.

"Noncritical Path Subprojects,"—however, may be shifted to the right, and in many instances overall efficiency will be improved by this shift. For example, while it is theoretically conceivable that "Personnel selection" could commence on the program's 30th day, that subproject is related to the restaurant's unofficial opening, a critical path event that is not scheduled to occur until the program's 178th day. Consequently, both "Personnel selection" and its directly related "Personnel training" subproject may be scheduled for commencement and completion on later dates than those that are theoretically possible. This scheduling is depicted in red, and it will be noted that the more closely a "Noncritical Path Subproject" depends on it, the more closely it approaches the critical path. This naturally results in subprojects that originally were not critical becoming critical, and indicates the wisdom of scheduling them with some leeway, the precise amount of leeway to be determined by the nature of the subproject and the judgment of Company A's management. Under any circumstances, however, Company A's management is prepared to develop its final scheduling of the subprojects that will lead to the grand opening.

This final scheduling is depicted in Exhibit 12.7, on pages 162 and 163. Again the key shows how to differentiate among the "Critical Path Subprojects," the days *scheduled* for commencement and completion of "Noncritical Path Subprojects," and those days on which "Noncritical Path Subprojects" *must* be commenced and completed if they are not to affect the critical path.

As has been mentioned, too, PERT-CPM technique is not only useful in planning a project and scheduling it, but also in controlling it as it progresses toward its completion. Thus Exhibit 12.8, on pages 164 through 167, depicts a control form that might be utilized by Company A's management to indicate clearly and precisely day-by-day adherence to or variation from schedule and each variation's effect on the project's critical path.

Finally project performance with respect to time and scheduling should be judged when the project is completed and the event "Grand opening" has, in fact, occurred. Exhibit 12.9, on page 168, depicts how this might be accomplished by Company A.

Exhibit 12.6: Preliminary Subproject Schedule Developed from PERT–CPM

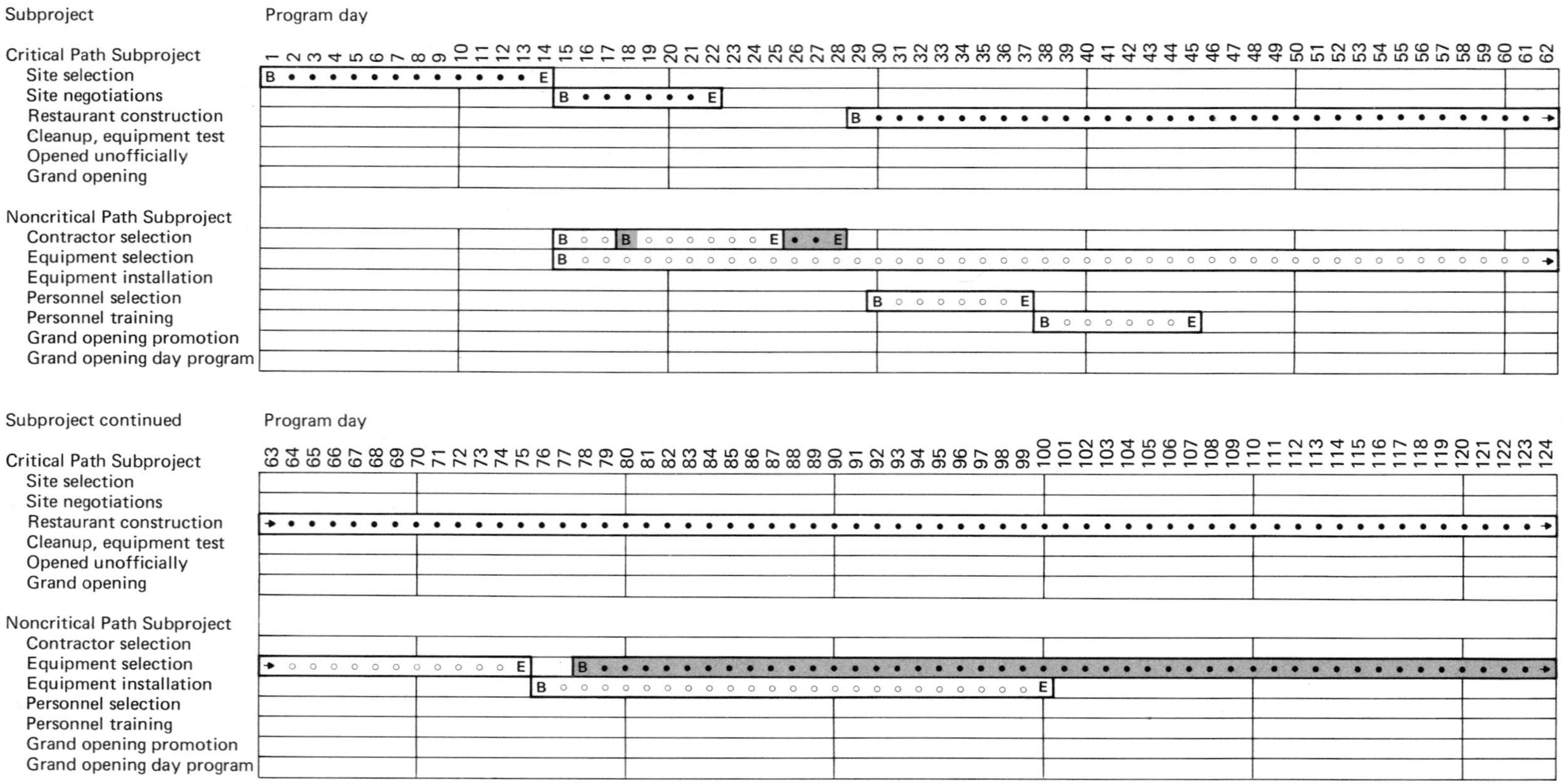

Subproject continued	Program day
	125 126 127 128 129 130 131 132 133 134 135 136 137 138 139 140 141 142 143 144 145 146 147 148 149 150 151 152 153 154 155 156 157 158 159 160 161 162 163 164 165 166 167 168 169 170 171 172 173 174 175 176 177 178 179 180 181 182 183 184 185

Critical Path Subproject
Site selection
Site negotiations
Restaurant construction ● E
Cleanup, equipment test B ● ● ● ● ● ● ● ● ● ● ● ● ● E
Opened unofficially
Grand opening BE

Noncritical Path Subproject
Contractor selection
Equipment selection ● ● ● ● ● ● ● ● ● ● ● ● E
Equipment installation B ● E
Personnel selection B ● ● ● ● ● E
Personnel training B ○ ○ ○ ○ ○ ○ ○ ○ ○ ○ ○ ○ ○ E
Grand opening promotion B ● ● ● ● ● ● ● ● ● ● ● ● ● ● E
Grand opening day program BE

Key: B ● ● ● E   Beginning ... End (or Commencement ... Completion) of

B ● ● ● E   Critical path subproject

B ○ ○ E   Noncritical path subproject beginning at earliest possible commencement date

B ● ● ● E   Noncritical path subproject ending at latest possible completion date

Exhibit 12.7: Final Subproject Schedule Developed from Preliminary

Subproject	Program day

Critical Path Subproject
- Site selection
- Site negotiations
- Restaurant construction
- Cleanup, equipment test
- Opened unofficially
- Grand opening

Noncritical Path Subproject
- Contractor selection
- Equipment selection
- Equipment installation
- Personnel selection
- Personnel training
- Grand opening promotion
- Grand opening day program

Subproject continued	Program day

Critical Path Subproject
- Site selection
- Site negotiations
- Restaurant construction
- Cleanup, equipment test
- Opened unofficially
- Grand opening

Noncritical Path Subproject
- Contractor selection
- Equipment selection
- Equipment installation
- Personnel selection
- Personnel training
- Grand opening promotion
- Grand opening day program

Subproject continued	Program day

Critical Path Subproject
- Site selection
- Site negotiations
- Restaurant construction
- Cleanup, equipment test
- Opened unofficially
- Grand opening

Noncritical Path Subproject
- Contractor selection
- Equipment selection
- Equipment installation
- Personnel selection
- Personnel training
- Grand opening promotion
- Grand opening day program

Key:

B ○ ○ ○ ↑	Scheduled subproject beginning or commencement
○ ○ ○ E	Scheduled subproject ending or completion
B • • • ↑	Critical subproject beginning or commencement
• • • E	Critical subproject ending or completion

Exhibit 12.8 Project Control Diary

	Subproject Commencement			Variation from		Subproject Completion			Variation from		Sch./Crit. Path Effect	
	Schedule	Critical	Actual	Schedule	Critical	Schedule	Critical	Actual	Schedule	Critical	Cum Var from Schedule	Cum Var from Critical
1	Site selection	Site selection										
⋮											⋮	⋮
14						Site selection	Site selection					
15	Contractor selection											
16	Site negotiations	Site negotiations										
17												
18	Contractor selection											
19												
20												
21												
22						Site negotiations	Site negotiations					
23												
24						Contractor selection						
25												
26												
27												
28							Contractor selection					
29	Restaurant construction	Restaurant construction										

(cont.)

71 Equipment
    selection

78 Equipment
    selection

131 Equipment
    selection

132 Equipment
    installation

138 Equipment
    selection

139 Equipment
    installation

156 Equipment
    installation

157
158
159 Personnel
    selection
160
161
162 Equipment
    installation

(cont.)

EVALUATING TIMING AND COORDINATION REQUIREMENTS

	Subproject Commencement			Variation from		Subproject Completion		Variation from		Sch./Crit. Path Effect	
	Schedule	Critical	Actual	Schedule	Critical	Schedule	Critical	Actual	Schedule	Critical	Cum Var from Schedule	Cum Var from Critical
163	Personnel selection											
164						Restaurant construction	Restaurant construction					
165	Cleanup eqpt. test	Cleanup eqpt. test										
166												
167						Personnel selection						
168	Personnel training											
169						Personnel selection						
170	Personnel training											

171	Grand open.	Grand open.									
	promotion	promotion									
172											
173											
174											
175				Personnel training							
176											
177					Personnel training						
.						. . .					
.											
.											
185	G.O. day	G.O. day				G.O. day	G.O. day				
	promo.	promo.				promo.	promo.				
	G.O.	G.O.				G.O.	G.O.				

Exhibit 12.9 Project Control Report

Subprojects	Schedule Commence	Actual	Variation	Complete	Actual	Variation	Critical Commence	Actual	Variation	Complete	Actual	Variation
Critical Path Subproject												
Site selection	1			14			1			14		
Site negotiations	15			22			15			22		
Restaurant construction	29			164			29			164		
Cleanup, equipment test	165			177			165			177		
Opened unofficially	178			185			178			185		
Grand opening	185		—	185		—	185		—	185		—
Total critical path			—			—			—			—
Noncritical Path Subproject												
Contractor selection	15			25			18			28		
Equipment selection	71			131			78			138		
Personnel selection	160			167			162			169		
Personnel training	168			175			170			177		
Grand opening promotion	171			171			171'			171		
Grand opening-day program	185		—	185		—	185		—	185		—
Total noncritical path			=			=			=			=
Total Project			=			=			=			=